PENGUIN BOOKS

AGAINST THE STRANGER

Janine di Giovanni was born in the United States in 1961. She completed two Masters degrees and was starting a Ph.D. in literature when she abandoned the academic world to become a journalist. She worked first for the Associated Press in America, and in 1987 she moved permanently to London, where she has reported from Europe, Israel and Latin America. She is currently a feature writer on the *Sunday Times*.

JANINE DI GIOVANNI

AGAINST THE STRANGER

LIVES IN OCCUPIED TERRITORY

PENGUIN BOOKS

For my mother and father.
And for Jonathan.

PENGUIN BOOKS

Published by the Penguin Group
Penguin Books Ltd, 27 Wrights Lane, London W8 5TZ, England
Penguin Books USA Inc., 375 Hudson Street, New York, New York 10014, USA
Penguin Books Australia Ltd, Ringwood, Victoria, Australia
Penguin Books Canada Ltd, 10 Alcorn Avenue, Toronto, Ontario, Canada M4V 3B2
Penguin Books (NZ) Ltd, 182–190 Wairau Road, Auckland 10, New Zealand

Penguin Books Ltd, Registered Offices: Harmondsworth, Middlesex, England

First published by Viking 1993
Published in Penguin Books 1994
1 3 5 7 9 10 8 6 4 2

Printed in England by Clays Ltd, St Ives plc

Contents

No foreign sky protected me,
no stranger's wing shielded my face.
I stand as witness to that common lot,
survivor of that time, that place.

Anna Akhmatova, 'Requiem'

List of Illustrations

All photographs taken by Marc Schlossman.

Preface

My brother and I against my cousin.
My cousin and I against the stranger.
Palestinian proverb

The West Bank of Jordan, the Gaza Strip and the Golan Heights became the occupied territories in June 1967, following the Israeli victory over three Arab armies in the Six Day War. From that time on the 1.75 million Palestinian people have lived under what the Israelis call civil administration and what they call military occupation. In December 1987, after twenty years of relative quiet, the *intifada*, the Palestinian uprising, erupted, first in Gaza and later in the West Bank and Jerusalem.

This book began one freezing-cold winter morning in Chicago in December 1987, when I picked up a copy of the *Chicago Tribune* and saw a black and white photograph on the front page. It was an image of four Palestinians in an isolated West Bank village being buried alive by an Israeli driving a bulldozer. They were lying face down in a field and the earth covered their heads and their bodies.

The caption said that the driver had been ordered to bury the men by the IDF (Israeli Defence Force) and that after the army cleared the area, the villagers had scurried back to dig the men out. It was the first time I saw the word 'intifada', which means a shaking that grips one in the midst of a fever, used in context with the Palestinians.

I was visiting friends in Chicago, staying in a wealthy suburb on the north shore of Lake Michigan. The population is largely Jewish, and the congregation of the local synagogue annually raised generous sums of money for the state of Israel. Many of the families I knew from that area travelled to Israel, where they stayed in the King David Hotel in West Jerusalem, and they never went near the West Bank or the refugee camps only half an hour away from their hotel, or even the Arab quarter of the Old City. They usually saw the amazing accomplishments of the government and met the mayor of Jerusalem, and they would comment that it was extraordinary how the Israelis made the desert bloom.

Even in Chicago, thousands of miles from Israel, the intifada changed some of that. People who had previously written a large cheque to a Zionist organization were picking up the morning newspaper and seeing the photographs and thinking, this cannot be possible. Jews cannot do this to other people. Or they would become angry and say, 'This cannot really be happening. The press is consistently anti-Israel.'

Some time after that I was reading another newspaper in another city when I came across an intriguing sentence in an article about the intifada: 'The Palestinian was represented by the Israeli lawyer Felicia Langer.' That same day I rang Langer and arranged to meet her a few weeks later in Jerusalem. She told me she had spent twenty-three years representing Palestinians in the military courts; one day she realized with a kind of sinking horror that she was representing the children of clients she had represented twenty years before, at the beginning of the occupation. 'I understand again that the one ray of hope in our terrible darkness is the angry voice that rises within us,' she wrote in 1988 a few months after the intifada began. 'I understand that in the face of such horror this voice will never be silent.'

Through Felicia Langer, and through a network of other people in Jerusalem, the West Bank and the Gaza Strip, this book emerged. I did not want to write a history book or a political treatise, or even to document the history of the intifada itself. I wanted to write about life under occupation, 'ordinary' life for 'ordinary' people, Palestinian and Israeli. I wanted to talk not to politicians and famous novelists and historians but to someone like Felicia Langer, or her clients, or the Palestinian teenager who thought nothing of stabbing a soldier, or the Jewish mother whose son was killed when his bus was fire-bombed.

For Palestinians in the territories, the basics of life are that Israeli soldiers and border police may enter Arab homes without a warrant. Palestinians may be stopped and required to show identification papers at any time. They may be detained without trial for up to a year. If they are suspected of illegal political activity, they may be put under house arrest, whereby they are forbidden to leave either their homes or their villages. If a member of the family has been engaged in terrorist activity, their houses may be sealed up or demolished. They are not allowed to fly a Palestinian flag, read subversive literature or hold a press conference without permission. They need to carry identity cards with them at all times; green if they have been arrested, red if they are from Gaza and orange if they are from the West Bank.

For Jews who are not too far removed from the intifada, life is constantly tainted with a kind of fear that anything can, and might, happen. Their car windows might be shattered by a stone, or their bus fire-bombed. If they drive in the territories, they either drive behind protective glass or take the risk of being stoned or struck by Molotov cocktails. If they make a wrong turn and drive into a Palestinian village with yellow Israeli plates, they could be killed. Thousands of ordinary Israeli children have been injured, and some killed, by the attacks of intifada activists. They cannot go on a school trip without armed guards.

I spoke to Jewish children who have never met an Arab and who cringe when they see them on the streets. They live defensively, in a state of terror. But worse than the underlying tension is the belief held by some Israelis that their society is in danger of disintegrating as they become accustomed to the psychology of the occupier, that they are living in a divided society as a result of the victorious Six Day War which asserted Israel's powerful presence in the Middle East.

This week, the end of the second week of June, is the twenty-fifth anniversary of the victory of the Six Day War, and the news from Israel is not good: recently nine Palestinians and four Jews were killed in separate incidents around the country, including a rabbi in Gaza and Helena Rapp, a fifteen-year-old Israeli schoolgirl who was stabbed on her way to school in Bat Yam near Tel Aviv. Two Palestinians were gunned down by soldiers in Gaza. Collaborator killings – Palestinians butchering other Palestinians, many of them innocent, who are suspected of collaborating with Israelis – are climbing. The Associated Press's latest figure, counting from the start of the intifada, is 593. Many victims were Palestinian women who were brutally tortured and murdered, sometimes in front of their families. The Jewish settlements in the occupied territories are growing – already there are 250,000 settlers in the occupying areas, including East Jerusalem, and more are moving in – despite Washington's refusal to grant loan guarantees if they continue. Reports are filtering through of a Jewish-style 'intifada' by far-right extremists and settlers who say they are tired of living in fear on their own land. Israeli police arrested 113 peace activists in Jerusalem who were protesting about the occupation of the West Bank and Gaza. Joseph Alpher, deputy head of Tel Aviv

University's Jaffee Centre for Strategic Studies, told *Newsweek*, 'Nobody in Israel says we had a better alternative in 1967, but the war led us into the present morass of occupation, intifada and a divided Israeli society.'

The intifada falters and wanes; frustration on both sides increases and twenty-five years after the victory of the Six Day War the prospect of peace seems further away than ever. In his book *The Yellow Wind* the Israeli author David Grossman recorded the following advice from a Palestinian in a small village in the West Bank. When I was driving out of Jerusalem and into the West Bank, passing by the new highways that are being dug out for Jewish settlers, and into the decaying camps and the ancient, almost forgotten Palestinian villages covered by olive groves, I would sometimes think of this and about how people continue to live under occupation:

Start thinking about us not as your Arabs, asses that anyone can ride, people without honour. Start thinking about us as your future neighbours. In the end we will be the people with whom you will have to live here and come to an agreement with, and do business with, and everything, right? It's not the Japanese you will have to come to the agreement of peace and trust with, right? Even if there are five more wars here, the children of my grandchildren and the children of your grandchildren will finally get wise and make some sort of agreement with each other, right? So I say: Change your attitude a little, make some effort in our direction. Even try – and I know that it is probably hard for you, right? – try, God forbid, to respect us.

Acknowledgements

I began to research this book in the spring of 1989 and in the time I spent travelling back and forth between Jerusalem, Gaza and London I have been fortunate enough to meet many people who kindly gave me their time, their advice, their contacts and often their homes.

In Jerusalem I am especially indebted to Natasha Fairweather and Richard Beeston, both of whom did so much for me. Thanks also to Roni Ben Efrat, Mikado Warschawski, Tikva Parnas Honig, Caroline Hawley, Benni Burger, Nabeel Turjeman, Ribhi al-Aruri, Professor Ahmed Baker, Maida Habash, Meir Grego, Dr Eyad al-Surraj, Quasim Izzat, Alya Shawa, Maral Kahvededijian, Yousef, Joyce Khalaf, Dr Cairo Arafat, Naser Atta, Laila Atshan, Veronica Cohen, Rabbi Jeremy Milgrom, Hani, Tamar Peleg, Asya Habash, Mary Khass, Bassam Shak'ah and countless other people who cannot be named.

In London thanks to Michael Watts, who first commissioned the piece on Felicia Langer for the *Sunday Correspondent*, my agent Anne McDermid, my editors Clare Alexander and especially Tamsin Barr, who laboured over the manuscript and my hideous spelling. Love to Marc Schlossman, who took the photographs and who really started it all, and to Shirley and John Schlossman. Finally, to Felicia Langer, who inspired and encouraged me throughout the project. 'I understand that in the face of such horror this voice will never be silent.'

Janine di Giovanni
London, June 1992

Acknowledgements

For permission to reproduce material from the following copyright works, the author and publisher gratefully acknowledge:

Joseph Alpher: excerpt from an article in *Newsweek*, 1992; Jonathan Cape Ltd and Farrar, Straus and Giroux Inc.: excerpts from *The Yellow Wind* by David Grossman, copyright © David Grossman and Koteret Rashit 1988. English translation copyright © Haim Watzman 1988 from the Hebrew *ha-Zeman ha-tsahov*. Reprinted by permission of Farrar, Straus and Giroux Inc.; Farrar, Straus and Giroux Inc. and Richard Scott Simon Ltd: excerpt from *From Beirut to Jerusalem* by Thomas L. Friedman, copyright © Thomas L. Friedman, 1989. Published by HarperCollins Publishers Ltd. Reprinted by permission of Farrar, Straus and Giroux, Inc.; HarperCollins Publishers Ltd and Little, Brown and Co.: excerpt from 'Requiem' from *Selected Poems* by Anna Akhmatova, selected, translated and introduced by Stanley Kunitz with Max Hayward. Copyright © 1973 by Stanley Kunitz and Max Hayward. Originally published in the *Atlantic*. By permission of Little, Brown and Co. Published in the UK in 1989 by Collins Harvill, an imprint of HarperCollins Publishers Ltd; *Jerusalem Post*: excerpts from articles, copyright © *Jerusalem Post* 1972, 1974, 1980, 1984, 1985, 1989; Senator Michael Lanigan: excerpt from an article from the *Daily Telegraph*, 26 January 1988; *Matara*: excerpt from an article by Boaz Ganor printed in *Matara: the Israeli Magazine for Intelligence, Weapons, Military and Security*; Ministry of Justice of the State of Israel, Human Rights Department: excerpt from *Derech Hanitzotz* report, copyright © 1989, and excerpt from 'Children as Participants in the Intifada' report, copyright © 1991; *Newsweek*: excerpt from 'A Tough Breed of Dove' by Angus Deming from *Newsweek*, 30 May 1988, copyright © 1988, *Newsweek* Inc. All rights reserved. Reprinted by permission; *The New York Times*: excerpt from 'Foreign Affairs: Time to Speak to Israel' by Flora Lewis from *The New York Times*, 9 March 1988, copyright © 1988, *The New York Times* Company.

Acknowledgements

Reprinted by permission; Observer Ltd: excerpt from article by Eric Silver, copyright © 1988, Observer Ltd; Penguin Books Ltd and the Peters Fraser and Dunlop Group Ltd: excerpt from *The Arabs* by Peter Mansfield (Penguin Books, third revised edition 1985), copyright © Peter Mansfield, 1976, 1978, 1980, 1985; Quartet Books Ltd: excerpt from *An Age of Stone* by Felicia Langer, translated from the Hebrew by I. Cohen. Published by Quartet Books Ltd, 1988; Simon and Schuster Inc. and the Jane Gregory Agency: *Intifada: Palestinian Uprising* by Ze'ev Schiff and Ehud Ya'ari, copyright © 1989 by Domino Press. English translation copyright © 1990 by Ina Friedman. Reprinted by permission of Simon and Schuster Inc. Published by Simon and Schuster, London; Swedish Save the Children: excerpt from 'The Status of Palestinian Children During the Uprising in the Occupied Territories: Part I – Child Death and Injury' by Anne Elizabeth Nixon. Published by Swedish Save the Children, 1990.

Note on the Text

The names of some people, such as the Black Panthers in Jenin or activists belonging to illegal organizations, have had to be changed for obvious reasons. The transliteration of Arabic and spelling of Hebrew follow the standardized forms used by the Jerusalem Media Communication Centre.

ISRAEL
AND THE OCCUPIED TERRITORIES
LEBANON
MEDITERRANEAN SEA
Acre
Tiberias
Nazareth
Nablus
Tel Aviv-Yafo
Petah Tiqwa
Ramallah
Rehovot
Jerusalem
Hebron
Gaza
Be'er Sheva
Dimona
Sodom
Yeroham
Sede Boqer
WILDERNESS OF ZIN
Nizzana
Mizpe Ramon
SINAI
RAMON CRATER
EGYPT
JORDAN
Yotvata
Timna'
Eilat
Aqaba
0 10 20 30 kms
0 10 20 miles
Tyre
Metulla
Kiryat Shemona
Nimrod
Mas'ada
LEBANON
El Rom
Quneitra
GOLAN
Nahariyya
Ma'alot Tarshiha
Zefat
Acre
Karmel
Capernaum
Sea of Galilee
Haifa
Mt Karmel
Tiberias
Yizreel Valley
Nazareth
Afula
Zikhron Ya'akov
Caesarea
Umm el Fahm
Beit She'an
Faqu'a
Jenin
Hadera
'Arrabeh
Qabatia
Misilliah
Netanya
Tulkarem
The Green Line
Nablus
Qalqilia
Ariel
Herzliyya
JORDAN
River Jordan
WEST BANK
Petah Tiqwa
Tel Aviv-Yafo
Ben Gurion Airport
Jalazon
Rishon Lezion
Ramla
Ramallah
al-Bireh
Rehovot
Jericho
Hizma
The Green Line
Ashdod
Jerusalem
Aida
Beit Shemesh
Bethlehem
Nahaleen
Beit Sahour
Ashqelon
Dead Sea
Kiryat Gat
Kiryat Arba
Hebron
Jabalia
Gaza
En Gedi
The 'Green Line' (Pre-1967 boundary)
GAZA STRIP
Khan Younis
Masada
Rafah
Be'er Sheva
EGYPT

1. From Here You Can See Egypt
The Gaza Strip

I walk between
darkness and light
the night of exile and
the shining memory of home.
The land I knew
is given up to strangers.
There in the sunshine,
do they feel my shadow?

Mahmoud Darweesh

I am in black within myself, but I always wear red for
my enemy.

Palestinian proverb

In the few months we had Gaza, we saw that we could
control it, but . . . there would be terror and we would
have to repress it . . . we have, without a doubt, the
power to repress it. But the question is whether we are
willing to use that power . . . maybe it wouldn't destroy
us, not militarily, but morally.

David Ben Gurion (Israel's first prime minister), 1957

A few miles outside Gaza, on the Israeli border, there is an
abandoned shack. It is white and set in the middle of a flat,
barren field, and someone has scrawled on the side of it one
word, spray-painted in black: 'Imagine'.

I passed that shack many times and always stopped to stare at it. I still think it is bizarre. Who wrote it? A left-wing Israeli, a dreaming Palestinian? And what is it they could possibly hope to imagine – life beyond Gaza, beyond occupation? I decided, in the end, it must be a joke. In Gaza it is almost impossible to imagine anything outside the hopelessness.

In Gaza the light is hot and strong, even early in the morning, the time before the heat rises from the sand. When I woke up in my room at Marna House shortly after sunrise, the light was creeping through the shutters, though I had bolted them carefully the night before. A circle of flies was poised on the ceiling directly above my head, ready to drop. I threw open my window. A very old rooster was below. I watched him, still hazy from sleep. Like most of the animals in Gaza, he looked miserable, scrawny, sick. He was pecking in the dust for something to eat, but found nothing.

The paint was peeling in the old bathroom at the top of the stairs and the linoleum on the floor was cracked. When I twisted the knob in the shower, one trickle of lukewarm water dripped out, not nearly enough to get the dust off my skin from the day before. I pulled on baggy, sexless clothes and tied my headscarf, and went downstairs to the long, dark wooden table in the dining-room for breakfast. Radwan, the waiter, who had been in the hotel for forty years, from the age of eight, brought plates of toasted pitta bread, soft-boiled eggs and an enormous basket of fruit. He has smooth black hair, which he constantly pushed back over his forehead. He offered me more food and kept giving me packs of rough Palestinian cigarettes called Farid. I smoked one, and drank two cups of coffee quickly while Radwan watched. 'You have a long day?' he asked.

I said, 'Yes, a long day, very long day.'

'Every day is a long day in Gaza,' Radwan said.

There was one other person in the hotel that morning, a German radio journalist called Peter who was doing a story on Jewish settlers in the Gaza Strip. He was enormous, and blond, with the sort of calculated Aryan looks that one would imagine might send waves of panic throughout the settlements. Peter had come home very late the night before, slightly drunk on Johnny Walker Red. Alya Shawra (who ran the hotel, and came from an old, distinguished Gazan family) and I were watching an Egyptian soap opera in the sitting-room. Every fifteen minutes she kept glancing at her watch and muttering, 'Where is this German? Where is this German?' When Peter finally stumbled through the front door at half past ten, banging the screen behind him, Alya leaped out of her chair and pounced on him. 'Where were you? I was so worried!'

Peter was startled. He scratched his chin nervously and said in English, 'I was only having dinner with Haider 'Abd el-Shafi and his sons.' His eyes were slightly glazed, and he had the air of an overgrown frightened child. He sat down heavily and tapped one enormous foot against the floor. 'It's just around the corner. Maybe ten minutes' walk. Very near.' Alya settled back into the chair and pushed her feet into her slippers. 'But the curfew! It's dangerous to walk around in Gaza on your own after dark.' She pulled another cigarette from her pack, dangled it from her lip and stared at him accusingly.

Peter said he was sorry. He brushed his hair out of his eyes and looked at me pleadingly, as if to say, 'Can you please speak out in my defence?'

I said nothing and concentrated instead on the Egyptian soap opera. I was feeling cooped up and claustrophobic because of the 8.00 p.m. curfew. It seemed as though I had been in Gaza for a very long time, and that night I had wanted to go out for a walk, but Alya had forbidden me. 'Go walk round the garden if

you want to,' she said. 'Don't go out in the street, it is dangerous.'
She had been edgy since the intifada started; as time went on, she
grew increasingly wary. The strike days were becoming more and
more frequent in Gaza – sometimes there were three a week, and
then one could not go out on the streets for fear of incurring the
wrath of whatever faction was calling the strike – so Alya had been
spending more time at home. Inside the house there was always a
feeling of airlessness, and even outside, on the veranda and in the
heavily perfumed garden, there was still a feeling of being trapped.

Later, after Alya had gone to bed, Peter told me that he had
been followed home to Marna House by a pack of wild dogs.
'And in the dark, with the dogs close at my heels, barking,' he
said dramatically, 'that was the most frightening thing. I was not
so afraid that someone would throw a stone.' Outside, the night-
watchman who slept on the *chaise* on the veranda moved in his
sleep and coughed. Peter was wide awake now, and wanted to
talk. He asked me about some of the refugee camps in Gaza. He
wanted to know if Rafah was as dangerous as people said it was.

I replied, 'No, not really dangerous, more disturbing' and told
him that he was lucky – at least he did not have to worry about
being mistaken for a Jew. I said that sometimes, as I walked
through the camps, tiny children rushed up to me, tugged at my
sleeve and called out, 'Shalom', testing me to see if I was Jewish.
If I instinctively said 'Shalom' back to them, I would see their
faces changing to show anger and hatred, and a certain amount
of triumph at having caught a Jew.

Peter was confused. 'Mistake me for a Jew?'

I said, 'Your hair. They would never mistake you for a Jew.
You don't look like a Jewish settler.'

He looked at me curiously and then crept up the stairs to his
room.

*

In the morning, after breakfast, I lay on the night-watchman's *chaise* on the veranda waiting for Yousef, reading a three-day-old *International Herald Tribune* and drinking still water from a bottle. The *International Herald Tribune* always makes me feel like an alien when I am anywhere that is not America. The baseball scores in Atlanta. The monthly rental of a flat in the rue de Rivoli. The *Phantom of the Opera* tickets half price. None of it remotely pertained to anything here. I threw the paper aside. The heat was beginning to rise as the sun got stronger and, with it, the stench of Gaza – the ripe smell of rubbish thrown in the streets, the smell of the open sewers in the camps, the dead smell of the sea, the flaming tyres that the *shabbab*, the young boys active in the intifada, ignited in the middle of the dirt roads to 'resist the occupation'.

I could hear Alya waking up in the back room where she sleeps, behind her office with the old worn map of Palestine before the partition, and I could hear the German slamming the bathroom door upstairs. He came down, miserable and red eyed, and said he had a hangover. I dived into my bag and gave him two aspirins and picked up the *Herald Tribune* again. The gardener had arrived and was hosing down the grass.

What is it about Gaza that makes it so hopeless? The matted scrawny dogs crossing the road, the heat, the flies, the dust? There are roughly 750,000 Palestinians living in the Gaza Strip, crammed into 440 square kilometres of parched cactus-filled land, bordered on one side by the Mediterranean Sea. There are eight refugee districts and neighbouring villages, teeming with squalor and overcrowding and angry and frustrated Palestinians. It is so riddled with troubles that after you have been there for a while, you begin to wonder why anyone wants to hang on to Gaza. In 1956 the Israelis invaded Sinai and captured the Gaza Strip, but they returned it to Egyptian control in 1957. I have seen old photographs of Gaza at that time, taken by an Armenian photographer who now lives in the Old City of Jerusalem. The streets looked wider, the children healthier. 'We were occupied then, of course, by the Egyptians, but it was a different feeling,' the photographer told me. 'Not so desperate. Now I never go back to Gaza.'

The intifada, the uprising, started in Gaza on 9 December 1987 when Palestinian riots broke out in the Jabalia district, and were then followed by riots in Nablus and other West Bank towns. What began as a spark in a refugee camp in the Strip ignited into a national movement. But the intifada has taken its toll on the people. After five years they are exhausted and worn out, and there are some who would say that the intifada, in fact, has ceased to exist. Now there is only life under occupation.

Of all the places in the occupied territories, Gaza is the most devastated, economically, sociologically, psychologically. The entire Strip has been under curfew every night since the intifada began and, according to the Gaza Mental Health Programme, thirty per cent of the population suffer from depression and *angst*; the forty-three days of almost constant curfew during the Gulf War were especially testing. There is a seventeen per cent illiteracy rate, and an entire generation of children are growing up uneducated because of frequent school closures by the Israelis or by strike days.

Houses of activists (or suspected activists) are often destroyed by the Israelis. The sight of the demolished houses, of the piled-up slabs of concrete in desolate lots in the camps, only makes the inhabitants angrier. Everyone wants to take your hand and lead you to see another demolished house. 'You see! They dynamited this and left eight people without a home!'

There is no way to leave or enter Gaza without going through heavy military checks, so Palestinians without identity cards, or those who have been in jail and have green cards, cannot leave and enter freely. In June 1992 unemployment in Gaza had soared to forty per cent, and many of those Palestinians who do work have to build homes for Jewish settlers. They are aware of the irony of their actions; they know exactly what they are doing. The cheap labour the Palestinians provide is called 'the slave market'. It is estimated that some 120,000 Palestinians cross the border in Gaza and the West Bank to clean toilets, sweep streets, build houses. A recent report in *Newsweek* stated that while the Palestinians struggled to get by on as little as six dollars a day, some economists claim that Israel has prospered from the profits of the occupied territories – nearly eight hundred million dollars each year.

If you wake shortly before sunrise and take a taxi to the bit of land just between Israel and Gaza, you will witness the most dehumanizing sight: Palestinian labourers waiting in a car park for Israeli farmers to pick them out to go to work for them. They are chosen for their size and their strength. They stand, hands in their pockets, smoking cigarettes, or nervously blowing on their hands to keep them warm in the first chill of morning, hoping that they will be selected to work for an Israeli on a building site for about seven pounds a day. Harim, who is twenty-five and has a degree in psychology from Birzeit University in the West Bank, is waiting in the crowd, shuffling his feet back and forth, with the other men.

'How can I work as a cleaner? In Israel? Because I am in need of money.' Harim shakes his head violently. 'When I was at school and I studied Jung and Freud, I thought I would spend my life in libraries, doing great research, writing books even. Now when I am cleaning a toilet or hammering a home for a Jewish family, I do not think of my dreams, of what I once was. I think of my ten brothers and sisters and my mother who are at home in Gaza and are hungry. I cannot think of anything else.'

Before going into the cattle market, the men have to produce electronic identity cards, which are fed into a machine by a soldier. Anyone with any kind of suspected activist tendencies, anyone who was has been in prison, anyone who has anything to do with suspected 'activities' is bleeped out.

'The economic situation in Gaza will go down and down and down,' said a senior official in Gaza with UNRWA (United Nations Relief and Works Agency for Palestine Refugees in the Near East). 'Everything is against it. There are more Palestinian refugees returning from the Gulf states, from Saudi, from Jordan, from Kuwait. And more and more work permits of labourers going to Israel are being cancelled for security reasons. I would estimate that from shortly before the intifada until now thirty to forty thousand Gazans have lost their jobs.'

To Israel, Gaza holds little strategic, military and even ideological importance. Someone making a case for why the Jews should keep the West Bank could point out the biblical history and sites, and stress the military significance, the fact that it is a buffer between them and Jordan. But Gaza is different. When David Ben Gurion gave Gaza back to the Egyptians after ruling it for one year following the 1956 Suez War, he must have realized it would be impossible to rule 300,000 refugees at that time, or perhaps he foresaw the impossibility of occupying Gaza humanely.

'In the long run, I don't think the Israelis are going to allow Palestinians to work in Israel much longer, and sooner or later the Russian immigrants are going to swallow up all the job space,' the UNRWA official said. 'Even if a political solution is reached, I don't know if an economic one will be reached. Egypt does not want Gaza. Israel does not really want Gaza. Who wants Gaza?' He sighs. 'No one.'

'Life,' said the man whom I had met the day before in the

service taxi speeding from Gaza city to Rafah, the town at the far end of the Strip, 'is like Zift.' Life is like tarmac, like shit. He was twenty-two, but looked forty-five. He worked on a building site in Tel Aviv, two hours from Rafah. His wife had just had a baby, his third; someone had got the message to him that his wife had delivered the baby while he was laying concrete slabs to make homes for Jews. 'The army went into one of the schools in Rafah and threw gas today,' he said to no one in particular.

'Were the children throwing stones?' I said.

He shrugged. One of the old men sitting next to him in the taxi wore a traditional white head-dress held with a leather thong. He turned round and gaped at me, craning his neck. He had a gold tooth. 'No. The army just wanted to make problems.' The new father stared out of the window where the army had stopped a group of Palestinians and lined them up, and were checking their identity cards. He snorted. 'What good is it now to talk to you? No one listens to us anyway.'

The hopelessness in Gaza seems to permeate everything. Of all the places in the occupied territories, it is the most terrible. It is not just the smell or the overcrowded refugee camps or the open hostility from the Hamas, the Islamic Resistance Movement, who threaten to turn the occupied territories into an Islamic state, but the sheer weight of despair. Then there are the collaborators, the Palestinians who, for whatever reason, decide to become informers, cooperating with the army. Inevitably they are killed by other Palestinians who take the law into their own hands.

There is a mural on the road leading to Rafah, one of the most violent camps in the Gaza Strip. 'You are called upon to tear the flesh of collaborators to shreds,' it warns. From March 1989 to March 1991 more than 165 people have been killed for suspected collaboration in the Gaza Strip. The Israeli authorities say only forty per cent of those were actually linked to them.

'Life in Gaza is a special type of life that only Gazans can bear,' said Dr Zakaria al-'Agha, a physician who was one of the joint Palestinian–Jordanian delegates at the Middle East Peace Conference. He was imprisoned for six months in 1988 on 'no charge, administrative detention' and fired from Government Hospital after twenty-one years of work.

'Why is life in Gaza unique? First thing, we are prisoners in our homes, eight hours a day from 8.00 p.m. until 4.00 a.m. Second, the schools are frequently closed by military orders. The soldiers are always on patrol, either on foot or in their jeeps, and they are free to enter any house. The streets are dirty because the services in the civil administration are not going well. On top of this, the people are subjected to tax. Even donkey plates must have a thirty-dollar tax.' Dr al-'Agha pauses. 'But the worst thing is that any person can be stopped on the street at any time by soldiers, insulted, maybe beaten. His identity card can be taken away so that he has to go to headquarters where he waits for hours and is humiliated, maybe interrogated. You want to know about life in Gaza? This is life in Gaza.'

This is life in Gaza. Sometimes in the early mornings, when I first woke up in Marna House, I would open my window and look out in the direction of the sea. There would be the sound of bells – a farmer walking beside his donkey on the way to town – and the faint sound of babies crying from the nursing home next door. At that time the air was still clear and not yet thick, hazy and blistering hot, and the flies that land on your skin and stick to it had not yet descended from their place on the ceiling.

I would try to imagine what Gaza was like fifty years ago, when you could see not a refugee camp only a hundred metres away but out across the palm trees towards the sea. Then the Shawras, Alya's family, still owned huge expanses of land and spent summers in Beirut and could travel straight up the coast, past Ashqelon, past Jaffa, past Haifa, until they got to Lebanon.

There is a sunken, decaying ship jutting halfway out of the sea near Shati refugee camp, or Beach camp, as it is known. I stood there with three Palestinian men in their twenties and a donkey tethered to a wooden cart. 'How long has that ship been in the water?'

One answered immediately, 'That ship is very old. It comes from Denmark and has been in that place in the sea for a very long time. Maybe as old as the sea itself.'

I turned to the second man who scratched his chin and answered, 'Maybe fifty, sixty years.'

The third man reckoned twenty-five years.

It made me realize that to the Palestinians time means absolutely nothing. For they have been waiting in refugee camps for forty-four years, and have lived under Israeli military occupation since 1967; they have learned how to sit patiently in prison, without any kind of charge, under some archaic military law called administrative detention left over from the British mandate; they have been kept in the 'banana' position (blindfolded, hands tied behind the back, legs tied with knees bent) for two days, a week, and in solitary confinement for three months, nine months. It is not the same kind of concept of time as mine, of deadlines, of missing appointments, running for a plane, making a scheduled phone call. The older-looking people never seem to know what age they are. In Shati I asked a man whose home had just been destroyed by the army how old he was. He looked baffled. 'Forty-two, forty-three, maybe forty-eight.'

His wife was passing by with a small child with strings in her earlobes instead of earrings. 'No he's not,' she interrupted, squatting down on the ground. 'He's forty-four years old.'

It takes her a while to work out her own age. 'I have seven children . . . I was married at seventeen . . . the army came when I was twenty, no twenty-one . . .' She counts on her fingers and delivers the verdict: she is forty-one, ten years older than me, seven years younger than my oldest sister. Her face is sagging, she is missing three teeth, her back is hunched and rounded. Everything about her seems ancient.

I am always conscious of the oppression, the heavy weight of time in Gaza, because I suppose on some level I am wondering when I will drive away and leave Gaza far behind me. In Gaza time means nothing because there is really nothing to wait for; only the steady passing of another day, another week, another year, and we are still here in Gaza, and we are still miserable.

'Life in Gaza is life under severe pressure,' said Haider 'Abd el-Shafi, head of the Red Crescent Society in Gaza (the Muslim Red Cross) and head of the Palestinian delegation at the Peace Conference. 'We have no protection whatsoever, we are completely at the mercy of the occupier. Imagine living your life with that kind of uncertainty. You can never plan. You can be detained at any time. Your house can be searched whenever. Your life can be turned upside down.

'Gaza is like an isolated planet. And visitors are like astronauts.'

Yousef was standing before me on the veranda, a thin shadow in the sun. I looked up and squinted. He lifted the *Herald Tribune* from my knees and motioned to me to follow him. He called me quietly, and did not smile. His expression was worried.

'We have to move. We have so much to do.'

Yousef was twenty-one or twenty-two, shy, soft-spoken, thoughtful and religious. When we were in the refugee camps and it was time to go to pray in the mosque at midday, he would excuse himself and drop me off with a family that he knew. Once in Rafah camp he left me with a family of about six women. Their home had been partially destroyed by the army, and what was left was one room where eight people slept and the outdoor partition where they seemed to spend all their time during the day. One of the sons was an activist who led wanted men into Egypt; he had been captured but had escaped from prison and fled somewhere, no one was really sure where. A photograph of him – a swarthy fat man in his early twenties – was produced. The house was demolished shortly after he disappeared.

We sat on woven mats and stared at each other. Most of the women did not speak any English, though a few had schoolbook phrases. The one sitting next to me pointed to my hair and reached out to touch the elastic band that held my pony-tail in place. She gestured to me to pull it out and then she took out a comb missing most of its teeth and combed my hair. When she was finished, she tied my headscarf properly, tightly under my chin and then back round my neck. 'Don't tie your headscarf like *Yahoud*,' they said – like the Jews, or, in Palestinian usage, the Israelis – which is under the chin like a babushka. They seemed pleased and brought a mirror for me to examine myself. Once they had shown me how to tie the scarf, they took it off and removed their own because there were no men present. They kept touching my hair and my skin and laughing. One sat behind me and watched everything I wrote in my notebook; she was a cousin, very beautiful and heavily pregnant. When she took off her veil, I saw her eyes were rimmed with dark pencil; she wore a simple gold wedding band and long gold dangling earrings. She pointed at her stomach and held up six fingers.

'Six months?'

She nodded and gently touched my stomach. Her eyebrows lifted in a questioning arch. I shook my head. 'No children.'

She looked stricken. Then she touched my hair. She said something in Arabic and one of the girls tried to translate.

'When I have the baby,' she said, 'I want her to look like you.'

Everyone laughed.

When Yousef returned from the mosque with the men, there was a scramble as everyone struggled into their headscarves. An older woman, so fat that she could barely bend over, rushed over to help me with mine. Then they retreated into the house and left me outside with the men. Thirty minutes later they reappeared with an enormous silver plate with a huge roasted chicken in the centre, which they ripped apart with their hands and fed to me, surrounded by rice with almonds, which they indicated I should eat off the big plate with a spoon. They did not eat with us, but left me with the men and sat a safe distance away, watching us or leaping up to pour more tea or to feed me more pieces of chicken.

After the food they brought cold cloths and washed my hands and face. I said I would do it myself, but they shook their heads and Yousef leaned over and whispered to me to let them do it. The father sat back and lit a cigarette and told Yousef that I was now one of his daughters.

'Maybe you want to come live with us in Rafah?'

The women laughed, though I knew they could not understand. I smiled. 'I don't think so. But thank you very much.'

'Not to worry. I understand. No one would want to live in Rafah.'

He was right.

We stood up to leave. The women circled me and tied my scarf again, kissed me on both cheeks, two, three, four times. When I turned round to wave goodbye, they were all crammed near the door, watching me go. The pregnant one smiled and held up her fingers. Then she pointed at her stomach and at me, and laughed.

Yousef was born and raised in Shati camp, but if asked where he was from, he would name a small village near the sea, near Ashqelon, not so far from the Gaza Strip. Most of the people in his refugee camp came from that village. Yousef learned English from the British Council and he spoke beautifully, poetically. There was a faint sadness about him when he said that his first experience of the occupation was when he was five years old, fishing in the sea near his camp with his brother. Suddenly they were approached by a group of Israeli soldiers. 'I remember them asking for his identity card and I thought, what did we do? We are only fishing.'

In 1988 Yousef was held by the Israelis in administrative detention for questioning. They suspected him of leadership of a PLO (Palestine Liberation Organization) group. He did not know how they got his name. He was taken, as most Palestinians are, in the middle of the night, tortured and beaten. 'The soldiers kept asking me if I wanted to be a woman,' he said. 'That is the worst thing, to threaten to destroy your manhood.'

Before 1948 and what the Israelis call the War of Independence and the Palestinians the *nakbeh* (meaning 'calamity', though they translate it as 'holocaust'), before the United Nations partitioned Palestine into two states, one Jewish, one Arab, Yousef's family lived simply and happily 'with lemon trees and olive trees and the sea nearby and everyone could fish for food. It was quiet and life was very small but very good.'

They left sometime in May of that year when they heard from neighbouring villagers that the Israelis were butchering Palestinians further north, in places like Deir Yassin. His family did not hesitate: they quickly gathered a few things and left nearly everything behind, following in the tracks of the Egyptian army. Yousef's grandmother buried her jewellery under a tree, carefully patting the mounds of earth over the boxes. She thought she would return to her house in a month or two, after things had settled down. She still finds it strange to think that they never went back to their village, and she still tells her children about the jewellery that is buried under some tree in what is now a Jewish village.

That same day they began to walk, the entire family and one cow, the twenty-odd kilometres to the Gaza Strip in the blistering sun. It took a few days because they were slowed down by the children. Why Gaza? Yousef, who has never lived anywhere else but within the cramped quarters of Shati refugee camp, did not really know. It was south and it was closer to Egypt. In Egypt there were other Palestinians. He shrugged. Perhaps that was the reason why.

From Shati, where his family has lived since 1948, Yousef can see the smokestack that is beside the family's village. It is not so far away, but from Gaza it could be another planet. Closer to the village is a wide beach where Israelis go swimming on the sabbath. There is an IDF training camp nearby; proud families bring picnic lunches and sit with their children at wooden tables. The children look bored but healthy and incredibly young in their uniforms.

I once went swimming at that beach after I had been in Gaza for some time, because the beach is lovely and the waves are strong. I ran and dived into the freezing, aggressive water, and then stood up; I looked towards Shati, towards Yousef, and felt profoundly guilty. How could I swim here when he was stuck, marooned in that desolate place?

Yousef has never been back to the village, but he knows what it looks like, what it smells like, the exact number of fruit trees and the spot where his grandmother left her jewellery in the earth. To him, that is home. He might say he is from Gaza at a border check and he has a red identity card, which means Gaza, but he still believes that he comes from that village near Ashqelon. Sometimes at night in Shati camp he can lie in bed and look at the lights towards Ashqelon and think, that is where home is.

I came back to Gaza to write about suicide because reports by the Gaza Mental Health Commission suggest that it is on the rise. Suicide is forbidden by Islam, and yet the despair of life in Gaza exceeds the fear that one will be condemned for ever in a blistering hell. It is the ultimate taboo.

According to Dr Eyad al-Surraj, a British-trained psychiatrist who is the director of Mental Health Services in Gaza, there has been a marked increase in suicide among Palestinians since the intifada began, and rates have quadrupled over the past three years.

'Many of the burn cases reported in the Shifa Hospital in Gaza are, in fact, suicide attempts.' These are cases where the victims deliberately burn themselves on the neck, head and shoulders with hot paraffin oil since it is available to them and Valium or sleeping pills are not.

In the Palestinian community it is difficult to detect a suicide because after the incident the family immediately begins to cover up, no matter how it happened. 'Islam sanctions life,' said Dr al-Surraj, 'so if you kill yourself, you go to hell. Like a Catholic. But sometimes you hear people talking about the desperation, and they say there was no other choice. Other times they say it was better. There is also this idealization of death as a way of conquering it. Death will be a way to heaven. There is a strong identification with the cause, the collective unconscious of sacrifice.'

Yousef was taking me to Khan Younis, in the southern part of the Gaza Strip, to the home of a 38-year-old woman who had committed suicide in May 1991 in the most horrific way imaginable. When life became too much to bear, Suad Tibi drank insecticide and then died, convulsing, in front of her fifteen-year-old daughter, Nisrine.

Leaving Marna House that morning, we passed a donkey pulling an overloaded cart. The driver was whipping the donkey furiously, but it refused to move, stubbornly holding its ground. A crowd of young boys, or shabbab as they are known, had gathered round, temporarily abandoning their stone-throwing positions on the roof of a nearby house to watch the scene. The angrier the driver got and the more he whipped the animal, the more it stayed in its place.

As Yousef and I drew closer, the donkey, frothing at the mouth, collapsed from the weight and heat and overwork, and the driver rushed out and tried desperately to push it up on its legs again. I looked at Yousef's face in profile. He was blinking very quickly and I felt something in me snap. It was a horrible and ludicrous scene: the shabbab shouting and laughing and pointing at the animal, the driver trying to lift the exhausted donkey out of the dust, the army jeeps speeding by and the shabbab jeering as they passed, the heat and the dust and the awful sound of the donkey as it hit the ground.

The donkey and that scene seemed to epitomize the decay and the despair and the sadness. Although I said nothing, Yousef answered me anyway. 'Even the donkey cannot survive this place,' he said. Life is like Zift. He flagged a service taxi, which skidded to a stop. I was the only woman, and Yousef put me near the window. We drove to Gaza town and then waited in Palestine Square until another service taxi filled up enough to drive to Khan Younis. We did not speak until we got there.

In Khan Younis the sand is grey and the sun seems even hotter than in Gaza town. Forty thousand Palestinians live there in squalor: five or six squashed in a room, sleeping on thin mattresses, no furniture, no running water, a hole in the floor for a lavatory. In Khan Younis one standpipe is switched on for a couple of hours a day for all the inhabitants' bathing and drinking requirements.

There was a hot, dry, southern wind from Egypt and we walked through the streets, deserted because the army had just been through the camp. We cut through alleys, past the houses dynamited by the army, trying to find the Tibis' house. No one seemed to know where the family lived, though when we mentioned suicide, people would drop their heads and shrug indifferently. Finally a gang of small boys playing in the ruins of a demolished house pointed the way: past the market with its stalls selling boxes of mouldy apples, heaps of nuts and dolls, coloured underwear, green and red lollipops and bottles of aftershave; past a barren, dusty field piled with stinking rubbish and goats; past groups of tiny children playing in the sites of the houses they used to live in, building play houses with stones and sticks. When they saw us, they ran and surrounded us.

Yousef pleaded with them gently: 'Go to school and learn. It is very important.'

A tiny boy took my hand and we knocked on the door of the Tibis' house. Yousef kept saying how shameful suicide was. I knew that he was upset, and had been so from the moment I told him I wanted to write about suicide. It is forbidden in the Koran, he told me. One day he came to Marna House with the passage written out in his careful, schoolboy hand.

The door, when we found the house, was answered by Nisrine, dark, small and intense, wearing jeans with a long smock dress and a white headscarf, Palestinian schoolgirl wear. Her eyes were enormous, ringed with dark lashes, but she did not smile, only showed us in. Behind her stood the grandmother, whose face was the saddest that I have ever seen: she had no teeth and her eyes were glazed with heavy blue cataracts. Her thin shrunken breasts hung down to her waist, and her hands were shrivelled into claws. Two of Suad's younger children sat barefoot on the steps leading on to the veranda. As soon as the grandmother saw me, she let out a screech. 'We cannot talk about my daughter! We have to be careful!'

Yousef turned to me. 'They won't speak to us.'

But I sensed that Nisrine would talk about herself, and that was what I wanted to hear. When her mother died that sweltering May night, she died in her daughter's arms. There were some whispers throughout the village that Suad had been a collaborator. I understood the grandmother's apprehension.

Nisrine looked at my face very carefully and let me inside the door. She sat opposite me and kicked off her shoes. I asked her about school.

She became animated, saying that she wanted to be a doctor, a surgeon in particular, but she was not sure that she would want to go far away from Khan Younis when the time came to go to medical school. She was the oldest in her family; at lunchtime she would walk home, a journey of twenty-five minutes, change out of her uniform and make lunch for her six brothers and sisters, the youngest of whom was four. She would quieten her grandmother, who lived with the family, from her ranting and raving as the army drove by in their jeeps. She tried to study, but it was difficult in a three-roomed house with six children under the age of eleven shouting and playing and tugging at her sleeve. Before nightfall she used to make supper and force the younger children to read. She took out her books again and tried to memorize *English for Science*: she spelt the words out loud for me and asked for help pronouncing them properly: micro-organism, fermentation, fungi, bacteria, vinegar.

'Always ferment the beans in vinegar,' she read in her singsong voice, 'or you can have fungi.' She furrowed her brow and laughed, covering her teeth with her hand. The little ones laughed too.

There was another room in the house, which was quiet and remote, almost peaceful, but no one went into it because it was the bedroom of Nisrine's parents. Her father was dead too, blown up in 1986 during an 'operation' inside Israel. The Israelis called him a terrorist, the Palestinians called him a martyr. A model of the Dome of the Rock Mosque in Jerusalem rested on a small table on their veranda. It seemed flimsy and lightweight, but the family treated it with great respect: a gift from the PLO, it had arrived one day shortly after their father died.

Since Suad's death six months ago her family had lived in a state not only of shock and grief but also of profound embarrassment and shame. When her grandmother was present, Nisrine could not even talk about her mother's death.

'Please tell me what happened.'

I was sitting outside on the veranda in front of the replica of the Dome of the Rock. Nisrine's younger sister brought me sweet tea and biscuits.

The grandmother glared. 'Don't tell her anything! She is wearing trousers! What kind of respect is that?' Nisrine tugged at her white headscarf and opened her mouth slightly. She looked at me as though she wanted to speak, but no sound would come out. The grandmother spoke of Nisrine, shrieking in Arabic. 'We can't talk about it! We have to be careful!'

'Why careful?'

'She died with her secret. That is all I can tell you. I am ill, can't you leave me alone?'

The grandmother began to weep quietly. Tears rolled down her cheeks and Nisrine handed her a blue handkerchief. She did not wipe them away and they dripped on to her black embroidered dress, over her shrunken breasts. 'She wanted to die and she died with her secret.'

Eventually, with awful persistence, a story emerged. Suad was tall, she was kind. She was a nurse and she was so clever, but she stopped being a nurse when she was pregnant with Nisrine because the local woman told her it was bad to work and carry a child.

'People still came to her from the village to get injections and aspirin,' interrupted the grandmother.

When she married her husband, Rosmere, an architectural engineer, she wore a long white lace dress and blue eye-shadow.

'She was the brightest!' shouted the grandmother. 'Always the activist. She was good at history and geography and she spoke English and Hebrew. And she was very good at embroidery and sewing.'

The photograph of Suad on her wedding day showed her in a dusty Gaza city studio holding her husband's hand. A slight shadow had fallen over her face. She was smiling and she looked delicate, young; her hair was very long and curly. Rosmere was wearing a dark suit.

'Were they in love? How stupid to ask. Yes, they were in love,' the grandmother said.

Rosmere was thirty-four when he died near the Israeli–Gaza border, blown to shreds inside a car carrying explosives to plant in Israel. Rosemere's brother, a 23-year-old Birzeit University student, had already been killed by the army the year before, during a demonstration. Another brother had died in Lebanon during the 1982 Israeli invasion.

Nisrine said that life after her father died was not as difficult as it might have been.

'Our mother compensated for us. She was both mother and father.' With that sentence, it seemed that Nisrine had violated the code and said too much, because the grandmother leaped up and shouted at her.

Nisrine dropped her eyes and tugged again at her headscarf. 'He was a good man, my father. He helped me with maths and geometry when I studied. And I remember going with him to get a check-up at the doctor's. He had to have an operation on his sinus, and the whole time he made jokes when the doctor put the tube in his nose. But he died before the operation.'

The night Suad died was the second night of the Muslim feast of sacrifice, 'Eid-al-Addha, which marks Abraham's sacrifice of a sheep after God spared his son. That night there was a clash in Khan Younis, between the shabbab and the military. Suad ran to her window to see and then walked into the village. Whether she saw or heard something, no one really knows. She came home slightly agitated and woke some of the family for a late game of cards.

Suddenly she began to pace the floor, and went into the kitchen to drink the poison. Within a few minutes she was in agony, rolling on the floor, screaming. Someone ran for a doctor, but it was too late.

'It was almost as though she had lost her mind, she was in so much pain,' said Nisrine. 'She was shouting, screaming. The children woke up and got out of bed. She sat beside the wall for five minutes and was quiet. And then, very quickly, she was unconscious.'

'We think that maybe she thought she was drinking water but drank the poison by mistake,' volunteered Suad's youngest sister, Hannan, who was twenty-four and newly married, and lived nearby. She wore a long dress like the grandmother and a headscarf, but also high heels, lipstick and a streak of blusher on her cheeks. Her theory seemed implausible, yet the grandmother nodded. But why did she kill herself? There was that rumour that she had been a collaborator with the Israelis.

I asked one of the local boys quietly if this could be the case. He shot me a dark look and said nothing.

'Perhaps she just wanted to escape,' said another local boy who had joined us. 'Nonsense,' the grandmother interrupted. 'It could not be that. She never lost hope. Having a husband who was a martyr should have encouraged her.' She pointed at me. 'It is forbidden to kill anybody, including yourself. And the second life after death will be the fire.'

Would Suad go to hell?

The grandmother shifted her weight in the chair. 'Yes, according to our beliefs.'

Hannan, who was sleeping at her sister's house that night, said that on the way back from the demonstration Suad had said, 'I have to do something. I know too much and they will make me talk.'

'She had prepared the poison for the trees outside the house, to keep the bugs away. But maybe she was confused, and drank the wrong bottle. After she drank, she lost her mind. She screamed and screamed and the children woke up. The children, even the little ones, saw everything.'

The grandmother, when asked, did not know how old she was. 'Maybe seventy? No, closer to eighty.' She came from a village near Ashqelon called Hamama. 'I hope to die there. We had olive trees, grapes and apples. It was close to the sea and there were many fishermen. My father was a fisherman. There were four of us. What a good life we had! To sleep all night without the army crashing through the doors in the middle of the night!'

As the grandmother told it, in 1948 she was, 'let's say, about thirty'. One night, shortly after the Israelis declared the state of

Israel, the Egyptian army came into the village and told them to leave quickly.

'The Israelis had beaten us, we had to leave the village, I took nothing, just my head-dress and my clothes. I had three boys and we took a cow and sat the boys on the cow, and my husband and I walked alongside it.' She stopped suddenly and pointed a finger at me again. 'But what happened to us happened because of you! The British.'

Slowly I eased her back into the story of her exodus to Gaza.

'It took two days to reach Gaza. All day and all night we were walking, and during that journey we passed dead people on the side of the road. Just lying in the sun on the ground with their eyes open. My husband put his hand over the children's eyes so they could not see, but they did anyway. They died not from the Jews but from exhaustion, no water, no food. The people had come from everywhere. They were running away. The Israelis killed my neighbour and when his four brothers went to get the body, they had planted explosives around it and it blew up.

'Then we got to Gaza. I don't remember why we came to Khan Younis, or how we got to this camp. Why do you ask me so many questions?' She blew her nose loudly and looked at me. 'It is just your way. It bothers me how you write everything in that book. What are you writing?' She made a grabbing motion at my notebook but missed and clutched the air instead.

'Then I had more children – eight children in the end. Now I have seven. The oldest boy managed to get his high school degree after eight years. He's not very clever. It usually takes one year. The other went to work for UNRWA, and another one is in Egypt. The youngest is clever, but he worked as a labourer in Israel and now he can't get a permit to work there, so he has to stay inside Gaza. He sells fruit in the market, when he can get it. But Suad was the brightest.'

The grandmother stopped talking 'Now you know enough,' she said and folded her arms across her chest.

Then a miracle, or so it seemed, happened. When I stood up, Yousef, who was translating for me, grabbed my arm. 'You've split the inside of your trousers,' he said in a frantic voice. 'Get Nisrine to take you inside and sew it up.'

He was desperate. When I looked down, I saw that there was a tear on the inside of my thighs and a small bit of skin was showing. If I had been anywhere else, I would have ignored it, but Yousef was white with horror. I stood up and motioned for Nisrine to follow me into the small room off the veranda where the family slept and ate.

When I showed her the tear, she understood and nodded. She took me into her mother's bedroom and out of sight of the grandmother she spoke to me, astonishingly, in perfect English. She took off her headscarf and I took off my trousers and sat on Suad's bed while she threaded a needle with cotton. There was Suad's hairbrush, her pink lipsticks; her cassettes of Egyptian music and a tape player, her books, her photographs, her clothes. Everything was intact from the night she died. The dresser was carefully dusted, like a shrine, as though she would walk through the door, sit at the dressing table and put on her lipstick.

Suddenly the door opened and the room was full of laughing children, amazed to see a woman sitting with bare legs on their dead mother's bed. Nisrine pushed them out of the door and shook out her hair, which was flattened by the headscarf. 'I wear a white one because I don't like black. It's a sad colour and I already feel so sad inside.'

She then began to talk slowly about her mother as she tied the cotton and methodically began to stitch my trousers. 'Everyone helps now. Aunts, uncles. But my mother was more than a mother to me. She was a friend. She taught me how to sew.'

Her manner changed and she became softer. She smiled. 'Now we have a secret too,' she said, pointing towards the trousers.

What was her life like? She broke the thread with her teeth and said, 'We do not have any spark of hope.'

'Nisrine, what happened the night your mother died? Was she depressed? Was she sad about your father?'

Her face altered suddenly and her hands flew to her throat. When she spoke it was more of a croak than a voice. 'I can't speak,' she cried. Her eyes were frantic. 'I cannot talk about it. Please!'

I said nothing. She shot me a look of gratitude and handed me the trousers.

'A secret,' she said. 'She had a secret in her head. Now we have a secret too.' When I went back to the veranda, the grandmother made it clear that I had heard enough. But Suad's sister remembered something that she wanted to tell me. 'A few days after Suad died, maybe four days later, a friend of hers called Adel had a dream. And Suad appeared and said, "Don't worry, I have died with my secret."' She smiled.

One of the youngest children flew into the room crying. The grandmother pushed herself painfully out of her chair and scooped him up. 'Now I have so many orphans,' she said in a tired voice, 'and all of them are Suad's.'

There was another suicide case in the Yibna section of Rafah camp and Yousef and I decided to go to find the family next day, but on the way to Rafah – which is at the southernmost tip of Gaza, separated from Egypt by only a high barbed-wire fence – there was trouble in Palestine Square in Gaza town.

Some *mulathameen*, or masked youths, had destroyed the apple cart of a Palestinian merchant selling Israeli apples, and

27

were dancing round him, threatening him with their axes. They hacked the cart in half and told the merchant that worse would happen if he continued to sell Israeli products. Yousef and I stood by quietly as we watched the merchant scuttle on the ground for his fruit while men stood about and laughed at him. Shabbab lurked in alleys; an army jeep pulled up and two soldiers jumped out and tried to chase them. But the boys disappeared into the darkness.

Yousef and I took the service taxi to Rafah, which has the reputation of being the most radical of all the camps in the Gaza Strip and the highest rate of collaborator killings in the occupied territories.

'Rafah,' said a friend of mine who had lived in Israel for some time, 'is the kind of place where they kill grandmothers if they think they are collaborators.'

In Rafah I got stoned walking by the mosque – small rocks that barely grazed me, but stoned none the less – and Yousef was troubled. 'It is the Hamas influence. Please, Jenin, don't think badly of all of us. It is only the Hamas.'

I told him to relax, not to worry, but an old man standing near the sign on top of the mosque that warns Jewish soldiers not to enter because it is a holy place glared at me and said something in Arabic.

'What did he say?' I asked Yousef.

Yousef shrugged. 'He is Hamas. He is shit.' When pressed, he told me the man had called me a daughter of Satan, the equivalent of a whore. In Rafah fundamentalism in the form of Hamas, the Islamic Resistance Movement, is rampant and everywhere there are men with small pointed beards and white skullcaps and long white robes. Yousef says you can tell Hamas by their beards; I say you can tell by the way they look at me – because I am western, because I am a woman, because I am not one of them – with animosity.

The Israelis define Hamas as a 'cancer called terror'. In an article in *Matara*, the Israeli magazine for intelligence, weapons, military and security forces, they are described as follows:

Knife attacks accompanied by the cry 'Allahu Akbah' are part of the understanding that the land of Palestine is the holy land, and that every believing Muslim must act to liberate it and cleanse it of Jews. 'Hamas' believes that all Palestine, from the sea to the river, is the noblest of all strategic goals. [Journalist] Boaz Ganor exposes the murderous and fanatic 'Hamas' movement, whose goal is to raise the flag of Allah over every piece of Palestine.

I went to the house of one of the leaders of the movement's security section in Gaza. It was the only time that I have felt uncomfortable in a Palestinian home. He would not shake my hand or tell me his name, he would not look in my eyes; even though he spoke English perfectly, he refused to use it, because it is the language of the West. He would not discuss the philosophy of Hamas ('Everyone knows, or should know, about Hamas'). He would only talk in veiled terms, using loose statements like 'the Land of Palestine is an Islamic state' and 'being Jews inside a Palestinian state is illegal. But being Jews themselves, that's all right. We are not going to throw them into the sea.'

He said Hamas started on 'December 9, 1987 – the first day of the intifada'. But he would say no more about the infrastructure, or from where they operate. According to the Israelis, the ideology of Hamas is a synthesis of pan-Arab Islamic religious ideals and Palestinian nationalism. 'The movement emphasizes the fact that the Israeli–Palestinian conflict is in reality a religious struggle between Islam and Judaism,' Boaz Ganor reported.

The Hamas leader's wife came in with a tray of fizzy orange soda. She was covered in a dark robe and wore sandals, and had a small child with her. She did not look at me and most of the men in the room did not look at her when she entered. There was a silence after she left. The Hamas leader cleared his throat and I was genuinely surprised when he offered me a cigarette. I asked about the role of women in Islam and he paused, scratching his beard. 'In Islam a woman has an important role, to take care of the children, especially when the man is in prison.'

He stood up and indicated I was to leave. 'You should go. I must wash before prayers.' He pointed to the door. I stood up and gathered my things. As I packed my bag, I asked one more question. How does Hamas feel about the use of arms in the intifada?

His companion, who sat in the corner glaring at me, frowned. The Hamas leader led me down a dusty hallway to the staircase.

'Basically, how can we liberate Palestine unless we do this?' he said and opened the door. 'But I am not going to answer that question directly.'

Yousef pushed me gently outside the door and into the glaring sunlight. 'Enough,' he said.

In Rafah camp the army is always present, always moving, more so even than Hamas. On the day we came to see the suicide family there were four jeeps with soldiers in protective riot-gear helmets, and Yousef and I had to hide in alleys and taxis so they would not see me and throw me out of the camp on the false claim that it was a closed military zone. We waited, sweating, in a taxi until they sped off after a shabbab who hurled a stone from a slingshot. Then we jumped out of the car and ran in the direction of the mosque, down another alley and into a small white nondescript house where Ehsan Abu Ubeid had lived. He died in 1988, in the first days of the intifada, at the age of twenty-two. When his father forbade him to go to a demonstration in the camp because he feared his son would be hurt, Ehsan poured kerosene over his body, lit a match and ran down the street screaming, 'Allahu Akbah', and his father fell by his side, weeping.

'My son was dying in front of my eyes, what do you think I felt when I could do nothing?'

Someone brought a car and they rushed him to Al-Ahli Arab Hospital in Gaza. Ninety per cent of his body was covered in severe burns. The medical report issued that day by the Israeli civil administration stated that Ehsan died of cardiac arrest and electrolyte inhalation.

He was, said his father, one of Rafah's strongest resistance leaders, a member of Fatah, the mainstream group in the PLO. He was first arrested in February 1988 after someone gave his name during an interrogation process; having been taken in the middle of the night to Ansar 2 prison in Gaza, he was detained for four months. In the first few days, according to his father, Ehsan was tortured and interrogated.

'But he refused to obey orders from the soldiers. He was the leader of his tent. During the jail strikes he was always in front.' The father suddenly paused, coughed and pointed at my notebook. He said in a shaky voice that my writing made him nervous. What if the Yahoud saw it, and then Yasser, his other son who was also active, would be in trouble. I laid my pen down and gestured for him to continue. Yousef spoke to him reassuringly. The old man held up one hand. 'OK, I will tell you.'

When Ehsan was released from prison in June 1988, his father noticed a change in his son. 'He was nervous, tense and angry. He used to talk about how he was tortured in prison, how they would take him to the sea in the middle of the night, in winter, and force him into the water with no clothes on, and then laugh at him. And they would put the hood on his head, but tight so that he could not breathe. He became very defiant after that.'

Before prison, his father claimed, Ehsan was 'normal, quite happy'. He worked as a labourer in Israel, crossing the border every day, and brought money home to the family.

On the day that he died, curiously enough, two days before the feast of 'Eid-al-Addha, he brought 1,003 shekels home to his mother.

'I asked him,' she said, 'when he would find a wife. Then he would not have to bring money home to me. Ehsan scoffed and said that he would never marry because of the intifada. He said there was no point, that he would only be imprisoned again and again.'

That day the family went to visit some relations in Beach camp. They slaughtered a lamb to celebrate the feast and then they heard about the demonstration in Rafah. When they returned to their home, Ehsan's father spoke sternly to his son: he ordered him not to go and said the army would take him away again. He locked him in his room, but his son crawled through the window. His father came after him down the street and dragged him home in front of the other boys. Humiliated, Ehsan went into the kitchen and, standing beside his confused mother, doused himself with kerosene.

'He said to me, "Be satisfied, and don't be angry with me. Farewell, my mother."' She did not understand and reached out to touch him. Before she could, however, her son was racing out of the front door, striking a match and screaming. 'Then he was running down the road. Then he was burning, burning like a fire. Then he dropped to the ground and my son died.'

In Gaza town a strike day was called by Hamas, and strike days in Gaza usually mean some kind of confrontation between the army and the shabbab. The day before, in Rafah, I read the leaflet that was distributed in the mosque announcing the strike and forbidding Palestinians to drive or work or open their shops: 'THE INTIFADA IS OUR WAY AND THE ISLAMIC RESIST-ANCE IS OUR WAY TO DEATH AND MARTYRIZATION.'

Early in the morning, after Radwan had made breakfast, I crossed the grey sandy road to Shati camp and joined a group of shabbab who were staking out the soldiers. The heat and the stink of rubbish had not yet risen and as I walked through the wide streets with their old, shabby, grand houses I could smell jasmine and hear the faint tinkle of the donkey bells. There were no cars on the road because on strike days everyone is ordered not to drive. The Mediterranean was gleaming like some strange faraway jewel, but no one was swimming in it. Two Palestinian children sat on the beach near the water, but they were fully clothed.

Then ahead of me, right up against the beach, was the entrance to Shati camp. There were burning tyres blocking the road, and the stench of smoke. A herd of sheep ambled stupidly by the tyres. A small white Peugeot 504, a Gaza car driven by a Palestinian, went past carrying an old woman and swerved to avoid them. He was instantly set upon by a group of shabbab hanging around on a corner, near a closed shop, with stones in their hands. The stones bounced off his car, but the Palestinian driver jumped out and grabbed the nearest boy, half his size. He shouted something. The shabbab stared defiantly. The driver's voice rose to a higher pitch. 'I was taking my mother to the hospital!'

The boy he was holding, completely unintimidated, shouted back in his face, 'It's a strike! You are forbidden to drive!'

The driver shook the boy. An older boy stepped in and they scuffled until a man with a donkey cart separated them all. The driver climbed back into his car and drove off. The shabbab pelted his car again with a shower of stones. The driver stopped and reversed, then thought better of it and drove on in a flurry of dust, shaking his fist. Another white Peugeot drove by about ten minutes later, but a heavily veiled woman leaned out of the passenger window waving a white flag, which meant she was either a medical person or press, or had some valid excuse, and the car was allowed to pass. The shabbab were bored.

There were about twenty shabbab in this gang, aged between two and eighteen, but one, the leader, was nineteen and looked troubled when he saw me. 'Please,' he said to me earnestly, 'when you come to Shati, will you wear a long black dress? You must respect our customs.'

A younger boy who spoke English argued with him. 'She is not a Palestinian, and she does not have to live the way we do.' Then the younger one turned to me. 'But today you will join us and throw some stones?'

I told him I would find a spot near them and watch how they worked, but I would not throw stones with them.

He wrinkled his forehead. 'That's not enough. You must join us and fight.' He said he would recite something from the Koran for me: 'Don't be frustrated, don't be sad. You will be victorious if you are believers.' He looked at me. 'That is very old, from a battle. Now we are in battle.'

His name was Salah and he was fourteen. 'Do you like Saddam Hussein?' he asked me. He said that he belonged to no PLO faction, that he would never be part of any movement. 'I just want to be free to do what I want without obligations.'

He said that he was a typical shabbab and described an average day to me. 'I get up at about seven o'clock, always tired. I wash my face and clean my teeth and I carry my bag to school. I spend four hours in school. Sometimes after school we have confrontations with the army. I go home, have lunch, have a nap, do homework at four or five o'clock. Then I have a meal and my friends and I plan the confrontation. In the evening we go to the mosque where we have lessons, intifada lessons. They are always telling us about the occupation.' He yawned. 'At night we watch Jordanian television. That's it.'

I asked Salah if he knew any Jewish children. His face became angry. 'With the Jews there is no chance of peace at all. We want to kill them, all of them. And we want all of Palestine.'

Salah looked up, suddenly animated. An army jeep was approaching outside the camp. There was a shrill whistle from one of the leaders of the gang and everyone ran into position, except me. They called to each other, some on rooftops, others lying low behind walls. Everyone had a cache of stones. I was sitting with a little boy who told me that every week the soldiers changed. 'We know most of them by their faces. The worst, the most savage, are the border guards. They are Arabs, but shit Arabs. Druse. Not real Arabs.'

The little boy said that to fight the shabbab and their slingshots the soldiers now have a stone-throwing machine that hurls small pellets into the camps during demonstrations and protests. 'It is big and sits on the hill, and it throws stones down on us.'

When asked, the IDF do not deny the stone-throwing machine. Instead they say that the stones are small and harmless and that it is their own defence against the stone-throwing shabbab. They call it their 'intifada on wheels'.

The soldiers drove by outside the camp. The boys called to each other with whistles and cries of 'Abu Shabbab!' They hurled chunks of rocks and the jeep abruptly stopped. There were screams of 'Allahu Akbah!' as the stones flew. Two extremely young Israeli soldiers got out, looked around and got back in. The jeep sped off and the shabbab were disappointed. They lit a new tyre in the road and lounged about, bored, smoking cigarettes and showing me their bullet wounds.

One fourteen-year-old was eating a slice of water melon. He spat out the seeds and showed me his badly set broken arm. 'A soldier smashed me again and again. Bam! Bam! Bam! And I never cried.'

There was another whistle and shouts of 'Jesh!' – Army! Everyone took off and I sat down with the old man who owned the shop. We watched the shabbab in manic action as though we were at a tennis match. One of the old man's granddaughters brought out a baby and placed it in my lap. The baby had earrings and was watching the flames lick round the tyre in the middle of the road. A shabbab paused from throwing a stone and came over to tweak the baby's ear.

I asked the old man if he was nervous with the shabbab so near. He shrugged. 'It is completely normal. It's nothing.'

Suddenly it struck me: this was like a children's game, an interpretation of war, but this was real. And the shabbab knew nothing other than this, because they had never lived a normal life. There was nothing else for them to do than bait the soldiers and call out rhetoric from the Koran and attend 'intifada lessons' that they did not really understand. There was no point in thinking of life beyond the camps, because they did not know what life was like past the barbed-wire fences.

On Nasser Street a different group of shabbab positioned themselves strategically to taunt the army. They were disappointed when nothing happened. Time passed and they grew listless. When they became bored, they chewed bubble gum and practised hurling slabs of concrete at the fire to keep their arms strong.

In Rafah there was a man whom everyone called Fat Ali because he was massive, with rolls and rolls of stomach bulging out of his shirt. But he could still sit on the floor with his legs crossed.

He had one long fingernail on his left hand, which he called the 'picker' (I didn't ask) and he wore cheap, fake alligator shoes. He also had a car, and his house in the midst of the camp was not bad by refugee standards. He was about my age, looked older, and was married with no children, a subject he did not like to discuss. 'It's very sensitive to a Palestinian man.'

One day he was showing me his English books and reading the sentences out loud: 'Can you believe your eyes? Look left, you should see a duck's head, look right, you see a rabbit's head.' He wanted to know if this was how they spoke in England.

'But you know your friend Shareef?' he said to another friend, who was sitting cross-legged on the floor eating nuts. 'He is wanted by the army now. Red Eagles. And he is engaged.' Fat Ali sighed. 'This life, this life we lead!'

He said that things were getting slightly better, that the mulathameen were not so active because there were so many soldiers in the area. He talked about the Red Eagles, a group of armed Palestinian youths. Then he switched the conversation to the army.

'Three, four days ago, before Yom Kippur, about fifteen jeeps came in.' He shook his head. 'When I see the jeeps, I come into the house and lock the door. Then I watch television. I'm tired of the intifada.'

We talked about the Jewish settlements in the Gaza Strip and Fat Ali looked wistful. 'Before the intifada we caught one of the Jews with the curls and beat him, but now after the intifada we do not do things like that. It is a military, not a civilian, matter.'

After tea at his house one day he wanted to take me to see the fence that divided Rafah town in half, half in Egypt, half in Gaza, which was put up for 'security' purposes. We drove through the streets, swerving to avoid potholes, until we came to the six-metre fence topped with barbed wire. On the Egyptian side, beyond the strip of no man's land, there was an Egyptian flag waving and a family was sitting patiently in the sun. Egypt was fifteen metres away. On the Gaza side a Palestinian man pedalled up on a BMX bicycle. He dropped the bike and walked up to the fence, checking his watch. The family on the other side stood up when they saw him. He whistled loudly, and they scrambled to their side of the fence. 'You see, this is Berlin East and West,' Fat Ali said.

'You're late today,' shouted an old woman on the Egyptian side to the man with the BMX. 'What's been keeping you?'

'I had to water the tomato plants. How is my brother?'

'Your brother is fine, but your father has been suffering from a cold. Now we are all getting ill.'

The conversation went on for a good twenty minutes, interrupted only by the flashing blue lights of Israeli police who sped by on the no man's land road separating the fences. There was a long silence. Then the old woman, obviously the mother, began to clutch her throat. 'I can't talk any more,' she screeched. 'My throat is sore. I'll see you tomorrow.'

'Tomorrow,' her son shouted; he waved and climbed on his bike. When he drove by me, I stopped him. 'Do you come here every day?'

He said he did, and that his family had been divided in half when the fence went up. He had not touched his mother in that time, had not kissed her cheek, but he spoke to her every day at the same time. 'Eleven in the morning. If I do not see her, something is wrong.' Sometimes, he said, she brought the entire family with her and held his nieces and nephews up so that they could see their uncle.

'It is not so strange, really,' he said. 'Once you get used to it. We are all used to it.' He got back on his bike. 'From here, at least you can see Egypt.' He went back to his tomato plants.

*

In the Gaza Strip there are nineteen Jewish settlements, and in the midst of what was once a Bedouin encampment is the Palm Beach Hotel. To get there you can drive straight from Israel on the road that avoids highly populated areas, which, if you have yellow Israeli plates, is always a good idea. The hostility that comes from the Palestinians when you are driving a yellow-plated car is incomprehensible. Suddenly, just because you have yellow plates, you become the enemy.

I once came down to Gaza for the day from Jerusalem and, because I was not staying and was going to be in a Jewish area, I drove a yellow-plated Israeli car. At night, on the way back from Gush Katif settlement, I got lost and started to worry, thinking I was on the road that would lead me into Gaza town. I imagined myself driving into Palestine Square with a yellow-plated car and the reaction of the Palestinians sitting near the market, drinking tea and smoking cigarettes. I could picture the anger that would cloud their faces.

A few years ago an off-duty Israeli soldier made a wrong turn and wound up in a Palestinian village. Realizing his mistake, he panicked, reversed and hit a donkey cart carrying children. The children fell and the villagers attacked his car, setting it on fire. They dragged him from the car and ripped him to pieces. Before he died, the soldier, who spoke Arabic, cried out, 'I am a friend of the Palestinians. Please don't kill me.'

I stopped a Palestinian farmer on the side of the road and said I was a journalist. He eyed me and the yellow-plated car suspiciously and pointed in the direction of the settlers' road to Israel. It did not feel right, but I drove on.

Either I took a wrong turning or his directions were terrible, for I realized in a few minutes that I was driving straight for Gaza town. It was late and I was very tired. I had been at Gush Katif since early morning. I wanted to get back to Jerusalem.

When I came to a soldiers' checkpoint. I thought about it for a minute and then stopped to ask them if I was on the right road.

One of them stuck his head in my window. He had round gold-rimmed glasses and a surfing bracelet on his wrist. His English was not great. 'Wrong road,' he said. 'You want an escort? I'll lead you to the road.'

It was strange to feel relieved that the army was leading me out: the same Jesh that the shabbab stoned while I watched; the same Jesh that I had to avoid in Rafah so I would not be thrown out; the same Jesh that spends an indeterminable amount of money to keep the territories occupied. The same Jesh felt, oddly enough, like my guardian angels, protecting me from Molotovs and my windscreen from stones – or, a worse fate, getting lost and ending up in a Palestinian village. I followed the jeep and watched the soldiers turn their enormous spotlights in the darkness along the road, looking for shabbab. I thought of Yousef and felt he would have been profoundly disappointed in me had he known of my relief.

The soldiers left me at a signpost and pointed out the direction. They gave me the thumbs-up sign. 'Drive safe,' said the one with the glasses, who thumped the bonnet of my car. 'Now you see what we have to live with.'

I had spent the most peculiar day at the Palm Beach Hotel, which is near the Gush Katif Jewish settlement. It is a resort of orthodox Jews, opened in 1987, the year the intifada started. It is open all year 'because it's always warm enough to swim in Gaza', the manager, a pleasant Moroccan Jew, told me. It serves Glatt Kosher food, meaning strictly kosher, and there is an indoor pool with hours for men only, hours for women only and mixed hours.

Downstairs there is a conference centre and two different synagogues, one for Ashkenazi, one for Sephardi, with stacks of *sidurim* (prayer-books) and *humashim* (books containing extracts from the Torah) at the entrance to each. There are jeep rides through the desert where the Bedouin live, and the bare and faintly depressing rooms cost between seventeen and thirty-three pounds a night. There is a mock Bedouin tent where a real Bedouin comes at night and makes Arabic bread and entertains the orthodox Jews with Bedouin stories. It is so odd and surreal that I felt as though I had fallen asleep and woken up in a strange dream.

You must dress modestly at the Palm Beach Hotel. If you walked around in a bikini, you would probably be stoned by the black-hatted, bearded, ultra-orthodox Jews who come down from Tel Aviv or Jerusalem with their wives and children. When I went, it was the first day of the Jewish holiday of Succoth, and the hotel was packed. I could not imagine why any Jew would want to go to Gaza, the most troubled place in the occupied territories, for a holiday, but as the manager said, 'To come here, you must really love the place.'

The beach below the hotel, which is called Katif beach, is beautiful, with palm trees and beach huts built from grass, but there is something shattering about it. To think that, if you look slightly west, the Bedouin are living in squalor and, maybe ten kilometres away, Yousef is living in Shati, is disturbing. But the guests at the Palm Beach Hotel do not acknowledge this. In the coffee shop I ate a kosher toasted cheese sandwich and listened, in a state of shock, to a group of young Americans, New Yorkers judging from their accents, wearing *kipa* (skullcaps) and surfing shorts, drinking Cokes and eating eggs and chips. I could not help but stare at them, amazed. What were they doing here?

The answer came later, when I was sitting on Katif beach watching a jeep-load of soldiers. They left their guns lying on the beach, stripped off their khakis to their shorts and dragged surfboards out of the jeep. Within seconds they were riding the waves effortlessly and throwing Frisbees, like kids in California. Rafts were blown up and Israeli beach tennis rackets emerged. They all had razor-sharp haircuts, more punk than military. I watched them and another surreal scene: a religious Jew with a kipa and long trousers walked, fully clothed, into the sea. His wife, dressed in a long skirt, holding a baby, did the same.

One soldier stood guard, still dressed and holding his gun, watching his friends surf. I asked him what it was like working in Gaza.

He pointed to the sea with his gun. 'As you can see, it's not bad.'

'No,' I persisted, 'you know what I mean. Working in a place that is so hostile.'

'It's not pleasant.' He did not want to talk.

But one of the Americans from the coffee shop wanted to speak to me. He wandered over and sat next to me on the sand. He was a cross between a Hasidic and a surfer boy, with prayer strings dangling from his purple and orange shorts and the beginnings of side curls. 'Nice, isn't it?' he said pleasantly, motioning to the sea.

I shrugged.

'It's too bad, since the intifada no one comes here any more.' He looked at me. 'Or maybe it's better. At least it's not crowded. Not like the beaches at home.'

I looked at him in amazement. No, he was not joking. He was completely innocent. He really did not understand where he was, or what was surrounding him. He believed it was a shame that no one came to the beach because of this thing called the intifada.

I asked him if he knew what the intifada was. He thought carefully for a moment.

'The Arabs hate us and want to throw all the Jews into the sea. They want to attack us like they did in 1967 and take away our land.'

His name was Steven, he was twenty-four and studying at a *yeshiva*, an academy for rabbinical studies, in Jerusalem. He came from an orthodox family in Long Island and he was having two days' rest before the Succoth began. 'My friends and I all come from the kind of homes where we don't drive on *shabbat*, or answer the telephones.' He smiled wanly. His friends, wet from the sea, wandered over, Mordy and Adam. Mordy was red haired and aggressive. When he found out I was a journalist, he began his attack. He wanted to know, he said, about the Palestinians. I did not want to talk about it, because I could sense his aggression. Instead I named some books he should read by Israeli writers.

He spat out some sea water on the ground. 'I don't have time to read crap like that.'

I said the books were not crap. They were by Jews and were beautifully written.

Mordy cut me off. 'Let's cut the shit, OK? What do the Arabs want from us?'

I said, 'Why don't you call them Palestinians?'

Adam jumped in. 'There is no such thing as a Palestinian. They're all Arabs, they come from tribes in Saudi Arabia and Jordan.'

Steven, who was more thoughtful and seemed more mature, was embarrassed by his friends. He said quietly, looking out towards the sea, 'Why do they hate us?'

I said something about feeling oppressed after twenty-four years of occupation.

Mordy stamped his foot. 'Look here! If you step on an ant, do you do it intentionally? That's what we do to the Palestinians!'

He turned to Adam. 'All journalists are anti-Israel,' he said emphatically. 'Look at *The New York Times*.' He jabbed a finger in my arm. 'What do you think of Bush's decision about the loan guarantees? Ridiculous, isn't it? Isn't it?'

Mordy was standing, wrapped in a towel, gazing out towards the Israeli soldiers in the water. He did not wait for my reply.

'Look at these guys!' he shouted, pointing to the soldiers bobbing in the surf. 'Look at these guys! These guys protect us! They're more than soldiers! LOOK AT THESE GUYS! THESE GUYS ARE HOLY!' Then he got bored and, turning, clapped his hands at me like a seal. 'So, talk!' he commanded.

Steven said, clearly uncomfortable, 'Mordy, she doesn't have to talk.'

'What do you want to know?'

'How do they live, these Palestinians? Is it so bad? We give them water, food and shelter, and before that they had nothing. Before that they lived in the desert like animals.'

I said, 'Where did you read this, or learn about this? Is this what you learn at yeshiva?'

'Taught me? No one needs to teach me anything,' he said smugly in a thick Long Island accent. I overcame a desire to slap his spoilt freckled face. 'It's the truth.'

I remembered once sitting in a service taxi on the way to Ben Gurion Airport with an elderly couple from north London who also owned a flat in Jerusalem. The woman said, when she learned that I had been in the West Bank, 'But don't they have any shame? How do they take pay-offs from the government? It's a bit like being on the dole, isn't it?' She blew her nose loudly. Her husband, who had been a professor at a university in England, looked out of the window.

'They don't want to live like that,' I said. 'Who would possibly want to live in refugee camps?'

'They've had chances to get out,' she said. 'They prefer to live off the government. If they didn't, they would do something about it.'

I said nothing. Her husband continued to look out of the window.

She stared at me for a few minutes, not rudely, but not pleasantly either. She looked at me as though I were a pest, an insect, certainly not someone who should be sitting next to her in a taxi. Then she said nothing at all for the rest of the trip to Ben Gurion Airport, near a place called Lod, which forty years ago was an Arab town, in what was then called Palestine.

On the beach in Gaza Mordy dived back into the water, Adam read a book in Hebrew and Steven sat next to me on the sand. He apologized profusely for Mordy. 'He gets out of control sometimes.' He said he would like to read some books about the Palestinians (he said the word slowly, and I knew he was consciously trying to avoid 'Arabs') and to see a refugee camp sometime. 'But I still don't think that this is their land. This is our land, historically, religiously. This is the land of Israel, the land that God meant to be solely for Jews. It's something you could not understand. You're not from here.'

'But neither are you! You're from Long Island.'

He smiled slowly and dug his hands into the sand. 'No. I told you you would not understand.'

I left the beach as the sun was sinking and drove to see the Bedouin, who lived about half a mile from the Palm Beach Hotel, and who pleaded with me to bring them blankets or a tent the next time I came from Jerusalem. 'Because of the cold, the wind. We have nothing! We are so poor!' The Bedouin man was called Ali and wore a long striped robe. He moaned endlessly. About the Jews. About the Palestinians. About his wife, who sat in the tent glaring at her husband and me, as we leaned against the camels and talked about the new Jewish settlements and the new road that would link Israel proper with the settlements.

Like everyone in Gaza, Ali had his complaints. 'Of course, the Jewish hotel changes our lives,' he said, leading me away from the camels and over to his tent. 'We're Bedouin, we like to roam. Now, we need papers. If my child is ill, I can't go to town because I don't have the papers to enter the town.' He slapped some flies off his head and offered me a cigarette. 'We've been here twenty-five years and still don't have any land.'

He was 'forty-nine, no forty-two, I'm not sure' and had four children. 'Three born at home, one in hospital,' he said proudly, but one had Down's syndrome. 'He's backward, a little slow, this one,' said Ali, slapping the child round the ear. 'He doesn't talk.' The child's thick tongue hung out of his mouth and his legs were filthy and covered in insect bites. He stared at me, confused and frightened. I gave him a peach from my bag and he bit into it once, spat it out, licked the fruit and then threw it on the ground and ran away from me.

The sun began to set over the hills, pink, orange and gold, and Ali led me to a place on the hill where we could watch the colours settle in the sky. He cupped a match in his hand and lit our cigarettes, then patted the ground next to him and we sat in silence. The camels screeched. The boy with Down's syndrome wandered over with his sister, one year older, who was extraordinarily lovely. She looked at me with great intensity and did not smile. 'She is so beautiful,' I said to Ali.

'A real Bedouin. Trouble when she gets older.'

With the sun down, the wind rose and the hillside became cold. Ali gathered his robe around him and asked me again to go to Jerusalem and bring him back some blankets. 'The Israelis destroyed our house three times,' he said. 'So I built this structure for the kids because of the wind. I built it, but I don't know when they will come and destroy it.' He says he sells his goats for money. 'Life is difficult. The children must walk one and a half hours to school every day, but we are Bedouin and we keep to ourselves.'

I asked him about the Palestinians. 'Oh, the Palestinians,' he said nonchalantly. 'They want a state and they should have it. Everyone should. Isn't the world made of states?' I replied, 'If only life could be so easy.'

Ali was not frightened by the intifada, or even by the Gulf War, when he stood on this very hill, he said, and watched Scud missiles fly over Tel Aviv. 'But I stand on this hill every day, and something always happens. The sun sets, the sun rises. The sun sets, the sun rises.' He grinned. His front tooth was missing.

'I can't say I should be scared of wars. God brought us here and God can take it all away. I am not scared of Jews or hotels or new roads. I am only scared of God.'

In 1991 the Israeli Ministry of Housing issued permits for fifteen hundred homes to be built for Jewish settlers in the Gaza Strip, which would treble the Jewish population to about five thousand. Slowly, by advertising Gaza as a sort of paradise in the 'Western Negev', the government is enticing recent immigrants and other applicants to settle in the Strip. There is no shortage of customers, primarily because large government subsidies make homes in the occupied territories cheaper than anywhere else in Israel. There is also a flood of new immigrants to Israel – Jews from the former Soviet Union, who have been lured there after watching videos of the great life in Tel Aviv, and the Falashas, the Ethiopian Jews.

A new highway has recently been completed, loosely called

the 'intifada road', linking Gaza's nineteen settlements with Israel without passing through Arab-populated areas. It has not been a cheap job – Peace Now, the Israeli peace movement, says that ten times as much money is invested in roads for settlers as in Israel proper. There are now roughly 100,000 Jews living in the West Bank and the Gaza Strip.

The settlements are a constant sore spot for the Palestinians, who watch the buildings for immigrants who have just arrived going up on what they see as their land, and feel powerless to stop it. Shortly before the 1991 Middle East Peace Conference began in Madrid, Shamir, then prime minister, had this to say: 'All of our territories, the territories that can be built upon, will be populated by Jews until the edge of the horizon.' So much for compromise, for peace talks.

At the edge of the horizon, two miles down the road from the Bedouin encampment, away from the mad yeshiva students swimming at the Palm Beach Hotel, something desperate is happening. Palestinian workers are building settlement homes for Jews. The setting is eerie, there is a dead silence at the building site as they climb the scaffolding of the half-built structures, no sound except for the wind whistling through the half-constructed timbers and the roar of the sea, which is directly behind the site. In the distance there is a flat expanse of sand and in the shadows more incomplete houses of concrete. The houses, facing the sea, look like shells. Twenty houses in neat rows for a hundred Jewish people.

'It feels like my heart is tearing inside,' said one twenty-year-old worker from Khan Younis. 'I'm bringing Jews from the Soviet Union and outside, and pulling them in to our land. But if a person does not work, it is impossible for him to live.'

He said he was the oldest of three children and that he had grown up in one small room. 'If this plot of land was in Khan

Younis,' he said, gesturing widely, 'there would be eighty thousand people living here instead of a hundred.' He will build fifty-eight houses in four months. 'Ask me how many days I work,' he prodded. 'Take away Jewish holidays, strikes and curfew and I work two or three days a week. Not enough.'

His friend, clinging to some scaffolding, whistled and he had to go. He shook my hand politely. 'You know the worst thing about it? The most terrible thing is that we know what we are building.'

Sometimes there is nothing that can lift you away from Gaza, away from the desperate standstill feeling that the people are trapped on this strip of land, and the world has forgotten about them, and about their plight. Once, in the late spring, after a day spent interviewing children in Shati camp, I went for a ride with a Palestinian television journalist along the coastal road of Gaza.

The beach, unbelievably, was still lovely, wide and clean, and the sea and the sky were like the sea and the sky in the south of France. For a very short time I forgot we were in Gaza. The journalist was extremely depressed. He had spent a lot of time in prison and he had been tortured. He often told me that there was a way to turn off the pain in your mind, to slip into another world, where you were not in a room with a torturer, and then you were no longer a victim. He did not get embarrassed when talking about the torture, the way the bars were fastened above his head, or the way the soldiers put the black hood over his head and drove him around for hours in circles, to disorientate him.

'The important thing,' he would say to me, 'is that you must always remember they cannot break you. You must not let them break you. Even when you are tied with your arms behind your back for three days and they put a black hood over your head and squeeze it tight, you must not let them break you. If they ever take you away, you must always remember that you are stronger than they are.'

He said he had never cried out in prison, refusing to let the Israelis know the agony that he felt. But people who knew him well said that he changed when he got out of prison, he brooded more, he felt the constant weight of the hopelessness that is Gaza. 'I think that if he had cried out in prison, he would be better off,' said one friend of his. 'When you hold that inside, something freezes inside a man, and you can never melt it again.'

After the Gulf War he felt particularly bereft. He often said that he felt the world had completely forgotten about Gaza and the Gazans, that they were destined to spend the rest of their lives drowning in the depths of their tragedy, rotting in the grey sand under the restless sun.

His son and wife were in America. Twice he applied for a visa and twice he was refused. He had photographs of them on his desk at his flat, alongside a painting a friend did of his prison number. The Israelis never referred to prisoners by name, only by number, and he had grown to hate his. Then something strange occurred. He felt that number had become a part of him, so deeply, he would never forget it. Now he said that he had absolutely no hope at all. He would sit for hours on the veranda at Marna House, smoking cigarettes and drinking black coffee. He hardly ever ate.

But this spring day was different. We drove along the beach and walked in the sand and, even though we passed Ansar 2 prison along the way, with the tents full of Palestinian prisoners and the soldiers standing guard, it did not seem, at that moment, to matter. For a second, I actually thought he was happy. There was a young boy with a donkey on the beach, and across the expanse of desert was a cluster of palm trees. 'When I was a child,' my friend said, pointing south to Egypt, 'you could drive the old route, all the way down the coast, to Alexandria. The sea was more beautiful then. The beach was more beautiful then. It was a very long time ago.'

I said, thinking of the barbed-wire fence in Rafah that separates Gaza from Egypt, 'From here you can see Egypt.'

He picked up a shell. 'Yes, even from here you can see Egypt.' Egypt was not home, but in Egypt, he said, Arabs lived life without occupation. 'With dignity.'

'We could go for a swim,' I said, throwing a shell into the water.

He smiled. 'I haven't been in the sea since the intifada began. It's just one of those things. You don't swim because it seems too . . .' – he paused, searching for the right word – 'frivolous.'

'No picnics?'

He laughed. 'No picnics. No fun.'

'But you're only twenty-eight! You have to have some joy in life, anything. It doesn't take away from the point of the intifada.'

'You know, I try to tell you, or to show you, there is no joy in life. In our lives, anyway.' He shrugged. Life, I thought, seeing the face of the man in the taxi whom I first heard say it, is like Zift. Like tarmac, like shit.

There was nothing more to say. We got in the car and drove away and then something happened. As we passed a police check, instead of letting us drive through, two soldiers stopped our car and asked to see my friend's identity papers. This angered him. 'Why?' he demanded in Arabic, and the soldier replied in Hebrew.

The journalist answered back in Hebrew, the Hebrew that he had methodically learned from reading the newspapers in prison. 'I have done nothing. Why do you need to see my papers?'

The soldier walked to the front of the car and kicked a light.

'Your front light's out. And you forgot to stop at a stop sign,' he said and, grinning, went back to his post. My friend and I looked. There was no stop sign.

It was not that the soldier wanted to see the papers, it was the simple fact that he had the power to stop us, for no reason, and do whatever he wanted to do. The same thing had happened á few days before, when we were driving down the street and a shabbab stopped us, frantically, to warn us that the soldiers were confiscating cars down the road. The next day was a strike day and the special unit of the army would use the Palestinian cars to drive into the refugee camps, dressed as Palestinians, to recruit collaborators or trap shabbab. We did a hasty U-turn in the middle of the road. The journalist said it was not uncommon; they had already taken his car twice and used it in Shati and Rafah camps, because everyone knew his car and trusted it.

After the stop sign incident my friend felt humiliated. The mood of the day, which had, for five minutes, swerved towards hopeful, was gone. We travelled north, into Gaza town, in silence and suddenly at the side of the road there was an old, old woman, dressed in bright colours, squatting on the grass weeping. As she saw the car, she flagged us down and when we stopped, she climbed wearily into the back.

Through sobs, she told us her story. She came from Khan Younis camp. Her son had been taken away by the soldiers in the middle of the night. When she asked where they were taking him, they said Ansar 2. She started her journey to Ansar 2 at daybreak and walked in the blazing sun, and when she arrived, they said he was not there. Then she walked to Gaza prison in Gaza town and the authorities told her to go back to Ansar 2. At this point, she lapsed into an angry torrent.

The old woman got someone to drive her back to Ansar 2 and a guard, laughing, told her to go away, her son was not there.

That was when we found her, sprawled on the side of the road, crying. She wanted to go to Beach camp, where she had family. She sobbed the entire way and when she got out of the car, she kissed my friend and she kissed me and gave us some kind of a blessing in Arabic.

'It's like Kafka,' I said.

'It's worse than Kafka,' he answered.

My friend drove me back to Marna House. He did not come in. The next day, a strike day called by Hamas, I left Gaza, hitching a ride with a Save the Children van to the border check at Eretz, and walked the rest of the way into Israel proper, with my bag over my shoulder, effortlessly passing the soldiers, the lines of Palestinians waiting to show their identity cards, leaving Gaza, the camps, the beach behind me.

2. Life and Death in Jenin
The West Bank

Everyone who wants the intifada eliminated must understand that there are only three ways to do this: by transfer, starvation, or physical elimination, that is – genocide.

Dan Shomron (Israel's chief of general staff),
Jerusalem Post, 16 June 1989

The time that my enemies expect me to be sad, I will be smiling.

Black Panther in 'Arrabeh

There had been an ambush on the road to Faqu'a, a barren village nine kilometres north-east of Jenin, and the three Palestinians had been dead for almost a week when I found the spot where they had died after a shooting incident with the Israeli army. On the ground where they had fallen their blood was dried and crusted into hard, black rocks. Someone from the village a few kilometres away had used an uneven circle of stones to mark the site where one of the men had died after being dragged out of the car by his hair by the special unit police. There were three of us – Waleed, a nervous Palestinian journalist who worked for a communist paper, Hani, my interpreter, and me – and none of us said anything. Hani looked off into the distance, past the burnt-out fields where there were no cattle and no signs of life, and pointed towards the hills. 'That is where they were trying to escape to,' he said. He picked up an empty bullet shell from the ground, left over from the shooting, and handed it to me to keep.

In the distance, nearer the village, a Palestinian flag flew from an electric wire. It was the first one I had seen in the four years since the intifada began that had not been burnt to a crisp, or removed by the army, and I stared, amazed to see it flapping so defiantly. Waleed caught me looking at the flag and smiled. 'Welcome,' he said, 'to Palestine.'

On the other side of the flag, balanced on the electric wire, was a life-size effigy of a Palestinian man, called a mulathameen since his face was masked and covered with a black and white keffiyeh. The effigy was dressed in Levis and trainers, and held a fake machine-gun in one hand and an emblem of the Fatah branch of the PLO in the other. It seemed so real.

'It's been here for months,' Waleed said. 'The army can't control us in the villages. They're afraid to come out here.' He snorted loudly. 'Here WE are in control.'

Some dust from the road blew into my eyes and I coughed; Hani and I climbed back into the car. Waleed got into the back seat with two bulky Palestinians who came from Faqu'a and were taking us to see the families of the men who had died. We had to be accompanied or we might have been taken for collaborators or, in my case, a Jew. The two chain-smoked cigarettes, and tried to avoid contact with my eyes. No one said anything as I started the car and ground the gears into reverse, but I saw Hani holding something shiny and hard and black. He had kept one of the pellets of blood. He silently put it into his pocket. We passed underneath two more Palestinian flags hanging from wires. 'You are no longer in the West Bank,' said the Palestinian in the back; I had thought he did not speak English, but he clearly did. 'You are now in Palestine.'

*

I went to Jenin because I wanted to write about guns and life and death, and the way that the Palestinians regard death: not as something to be feared, but as something to be revered. I thought about it when I interviewed a fourteen-year-old in the West Bank one scorching summer day and asked him, 'But aren't you afraid to die? When you throw stones at a soldier, you're not afraid to get hit, or beaten up, or sent to prison where God knows what will happen to you?'

He looked at me, his face radiant. 'It is what I pray for.'

He was not afraid of dying, and if he was, if he had a moment's twinge of fear that that bullet was the one that was going to hit him, he would never admit it. Death had become incorporated into his life. He lived with it so closely and so fiercely that it no longer harboured any kind of mystery at all.

I wanted to write about guns because the direction of the intifada was changing, and in the refugee camps more of the young people in particular were taking up arms as opposed to throwing stones or hurling Molotovs. Four years of the intifada had worn them down; many had given up completely and the small resistance that was left was reckless. They had nothing to lose.

After the Gulf War the Palestinians, despondent and depressed, were fed up with the usual rhetoric from the Unified Leadership for the Uprising, the slogans, the useless demonstrations and the failed attempts to find a solution at the Peace Conference. They had gambled on Saddam Hussein; they saw him as the hero who would lift them far away from the misery of the occupation. They made a horrific mistake; the day the war ended and they realized that Rambo had failed them the euphoria they felt standing on the rooftops cheering on the Scud missiles soaring towards Tel Aviv was gone. In its place was a vast sense of hopelessness, out of which could come only desperation.

In the six months immediately following the war violence in the camps was a more common occurrence and the figures for collaborator killings rapidly increased. Inside the camps there was tension. In Rafah camp in the Gaza Strip early one morning with an English journalist I noticed a hostility that I had never encountered. Rafah camp is a Hamas stronghold, and even though the other journalist and I were both conservatively dressed and wearing headscarves tied round the back of our heads, I could still feel the stares as we walked through the market in the centre of the camp.

I fixed my eyes on my shoes, which were caked in dust and mud, my head dropped to avoid attention. The other journalist walked beside me, stopping at one of the stalls to ask directions to her friend Jamil's house. Next to her an old man was gutting fish behind his own stall. Two women behind us pointed and said, 'You see, they are wearing scarves. They understand.' The man at the fish stall, however, looked at us both with suspicion and outrage. 'You have no right to be here,' he said in Arabic.

My friend spoke to him gently in Arabic, explaining that we were journalists and here to see someone who lived in the camp, but he turned away. She shrugged and we walked on. Outside the market, in the fierce bright heat of the dirt street that is the main drag of Rafah, I saw two Israeli jeeps speed by, followed by a torrent of stones that the children, hiding in an alley, had thrown. We turned in the direction of Jamil's house, though not before I felt the first stone hit my back, softly, then another one hit my lower leg. A third one hit my arm as a group of children flocked around us.

'Sahafia,' I said quietly to them, Arabic for journalists, and motioned for them to go away, but they trailed us the entire way to Jamil's house, shouting and throwing tiny stones. It was not particularly dangerous, and the stones did not hurt; it was just the tone of the encounter. Those children were angry. They did not want us to be in their camp. It was the first time I had felt that in a refugee camp.

Inside Jamil's house we sat on the floor. He poured tea in small cups. 'Things aren't the same as they used to be,' he said. 'They used to be happy to see you, to talk to journalists because they thought that you could change things. Remember how much hope there was at the beginning of the intifada? Now things are different. They're suspicious of everyone.'

Things had changed since the Gulf War. People were more wary, and new youth factions of the PLO were springing up with names like baseball teams: the Red Eagles, the Black Panthers. They were secret groups who patrolled the camps and the villages, usually at night, killing collaborators, writing slogans, training new recruits and building up their arms caches. They were not easy to find; most of them had been captured by the IDF or were wanted men and on the run. But someone told me that the best place to find them and see them working was Jenin, a city in the north of the West Bank that had been active throughout the intifada. Jenin had replaced Nablus as the hub of underground activity.

Jenin is about half an hour north of Nablus, deep in rural countryside that is remote and green, with more villages and small farming communities than camps. The country outside the town changes quickly: from lush farming hills to bleak fields lined with scrawny cactus. Inside, the town has the same decrepit ambience as Nablus: crowded market streets clotted with rotted fruits and vegetables; the smell of stale bread and open sewage and thick cigarettes and coffee and anise seeds and leaded petrol; buildings masked in angry red intifada slogans; demolished, destroyed skeleton structures; half-starved dogs running through the streets, children crying, everywhere the air of sadness and desolation.

As Jenin is more difficult for the army to control because of the surrounding isolated villages, it is teeming with underground activities.

The three men who died on the road to Faqu'a are now martyrs, heroes of the intifada, but two weeks ago they were members of the Black Panthers, a group of armed youths who pledged their allegiance to the Fatah arm of the PLO. Each village has a PLO faction stronghold, and in Faqu'a it is Fatah, the mainstream group in the PLO. One of the shabbab was seventeen years old, the other two were in their early twenties. They had been on the run for the past three weeks because they were wanted by the army in connection with the murder on 14 September 1991 of a twenty-year-old Israeli soldier called Yoram Cohen in the nearby village of Misilliah.

The IDF told me that Sergeant Cohen had been 'killed in a clash yesterday between IDF patrol and terrorists'. They said a number of bullets were fired from an ambush at the edge of an olive grove, near a farmhouse, at the mobile IDF patrol which was on operational duty in Misilliah. The soldiers fired back at the source of the shots and in the midst of the clash Cohen was killed. Six bullet shells were found from a Kalashnikov gun and Cohen became another statistic: in October 1991 he was the eleventh soldier to have been killed in the West Bank and Gaza since the intifada began; 1,730 soldiers had been injured.

Some of the shabbab's comrades said that the soldier had been killed as an act of revenge. Another Black Panther had died, a few months before, after a clash with the army. 'He was shot in the leg during an ambush,' said Waleed, twitching in the back seat. 'And died later during interrogation.'

I have heard this phrase so often – 'he died during interrogation' – that I am sometimes embarrassed by my lack of reaction.

'How did your son die?' I would ask a woman in Beach camp in Gaza or Jalazon in the West Bank or Deheishe near Bethlehem, and the answer is nearly always the same: 'He died during interrogation.' No one ever throws stones. No one is ever involved in an act of terrorism. No one is ever actively trying to harm innocent Israelis, because to them there are no innocent Israelis; they see them only as the occupier, as the stranger who took over their land. I thought briefly of what one Israeli soldier told me in a weary voice. 'Every old woman who dies of a heart attack in a refugee camp during a raid is said to be a victim of the intifada. You can't blame us for everything.'

I asked Waleed if the soldier was murdered in retribution for the killing of the Black Panther. Hani, who is a Christian Palestinian from Ramallah, intelligent and sensitive, is not nearly as radical as some of his comrades. Still, he flinched slightly and looked at me sharply out of the corner of his eye. 'Don't say murder,' he said quietly. 'Please don't say murder. This is not the same as murder. This is the intifada, this is the way people live.'

Life seemed cheap in Palestine. We drove a short distance from the ambush spot into Faqu'a past the piles of stinking rubbish, past the cemetery where other martyrs were buried, dodging the gaping, unfilled holes in the road that shook my car. I stalled twice and while I was gunning the engine and cursing the useless Fiat, Waleed said that the Israelis refused to fill the potholes 'because Jewish settlers don't use this road, so why should they?' The two large Palestinians in the back poked him to repeat what he said, and after he did so, in Arabic, one of them launched into an impassioned monologue on the fact that they paid taxes too, and what did they get for it? Curfew, school closures and harassment.

Waleed was beginning to annoy me. He kept tugging on my

sleeve as he translated every complaint. 'Write this down! Write this down!' he shouted at me. I said I had enough information. 'No, you haven't. You must write this down.' When I refused, he would sulk.

Before we entered the village, Hani tapped me gently on the shoulder and asked me to swap places and let him drive with Waleed sitting next to him. I was to go in the back, between the two Palestinians, where I was less conspicuous; villagers would be less likely to take me for Shin Bet, the Israeli domestic secret police, and them for collaborators. We pulled up next to a graveyard of broken-down cars and piled out, rearranged ourselves and got back in. I squeezed between the two men, conscious of not touching any part of my body against theirs. Suddenly I realized I was in the middle of nowhere, somewhere in the northernmost part of the West Bank, in a Palestinian village with four activists whom I did not know.

One of the Palestinians tried to be friendly. He produced a packet of English cigarettes and the other man lit one for me.

The one on my right asked Hani what my name was.

'Her name,' Hani answered, 'is Janine.'

'Janine?' the one on the left said quizzically. 'But how can this be? It is an Arabic name.'

The one on the right turned and said to me in Arabic, 'It is the name of our town, Jenin, you know Jenin?'

'I know Jenin,' I said.

'It means new-born baby.'

I told him that it actually meant foetus, not new-born baby, and there was an uncomfortable silence in the car before one of them said something quickly in Arabic. Hani blanched. Everyone else laughed.

Inside Faqu'a it was the second day of mourning for one of the boys, Sab'r Muhammed Abu Farhu, who had died. A high wind was rising from the east, a hot wind, and it was as dusty in the village as it had been on the road. It was mid-afternoon, the sun was at its height and everyone was inside the whitewashed houses. The street was empty of children, and only a few women covered in dark cloth were to be seen on their way to sit with Sab'r's mother and two sisters, who were mourning with the women, separately from the father and brothers.

We drove through streets so narrow that the car could barely pass through, scraping white paint off the side of the doors. Old men sitting in a doorway glanced up at us, saw the blue West Bank licence plates and looked down again. When they saw me wedged in between the two men in the back, they appeared confused. We stopped to ask directions and the Palestinian on my right who had given me the cigarette said something to Hani. Hani turned round and said, 'That old man was a collaborator.'

'How do you know that?' I said.

He shrugged.

There were more fresh slogans in red paint on the walls, the same ones that I had seen earlier on: 'Sab'r, from the spark of your death we will light a new intifada'; 'Sab'r was killed and his soul is going around the intifada.' Out of the corner of my eye I saw a small child, about eight years old, wearing a keffiyeh and writing on one of the walls with a spray-can of paint. He was so short that he could barely reach the middle of the wall, and when he saw me, he dropped the can and ran. Another Palestinian from the village squeezed into the car and we drove through tiny, winding streets to the empty house where Sab'r's father and his four brothers and what seemed to be an uncountable number of relatives were holding the wake.

The house was set on the edge of a brown fallow field and there was a goat and a rusty bicycle outside. It was squat and concrete and depressing. Waleed went inside first to ask permission to bring me, a woman, into the room. He was gone for a few minutes and then came ambling slowly back to the car and instructed me to put my headscarf back on. I tied it carefully, tucking all my hair underneath, and pulled my long shirt outside my jeans. The only part of me that was exposed was my hands.

I was still not entirely prepared for the scene inside. The room was bare, with a concrete floor and walls and no furniture except for a single row of chairs around the perimeter of the room. On the chairs sat an army of men with black beards. They looked angry, sad, frustrated, and when they saw me, their expressions changed to confusion, then annoyance, then back to confusion. I was the only woman, I was not a Muslim and I was wearing trousers. I had the oddest sensation, walking across the room and taking my seat. Forty pairs of eyes took into account every detail of my dress, my face, my body. There was a dead silence until one of the men shouted to Hani to take me away.

He rushed over to the man and tried to explain. 'She is a journalist, she's writing about Sab'r . . .'

The man held up one hand in front of his face and waved Hani away. Hani sat next to me.

'It will be ·OK,' he said and lit a cigarette. The men sitting in the chairs opposite stared at me, unabashed. When I met their stares, they did not look away.

One of Sab'r's brothers approached us.

'Don't shake his hand,' Hani hissed. 'He's religious.'

My hand dangled uselessly at my side as I introduced myself and then sat down again carefully, without crossing my legs, conscious that someone once told me it is rude to show the soles of your feet to an Arab. The wind whistled through the empty room, breaking the awkward silence. Someone brought me a tiny cup of black sweetened coffee from an urn and urged me to drink it quickly, in one swallow. Then they poured for Hani and for Waleed. I leaned over and asked Hani if I could smoke.

'You can do what you want,' he said. But he looked faintly nervous. His foot twitched. 'Are you afraid?'

I told him that I felt uncomfortable. He looked troubled.

'Uncomfortable? That means that you don't trust me. Do you think I would let anything happen to you?'

'No. It's not that.'

He had misunderstood me. To him, being in the midst of Faqu'a's Fatah stronghold was the greatest honour one would ask for. Here was a martyr's family, I was invited to their Beit al-'Azza (house of mourning), and I was uncomfortable. Worse was the fact that I had in some way offended his masculine pride. He was supposed to be looking out for me and yet I felt uneasy. I had doubted him.

'Have a cigarette,' I said and he grudgingly took it. He allowed me to light the match, an act that did not go unnoticed in the silent room.

The men all wore cheap grey trousers, blue button-down shirts and sandals. If I looked across the room quickly, all I could see was a blur of muted colours – grey and blue – and black beards. We sat without talking for a few minutes before we were called into a private audience with Sab'r's father. I felt an instant relief the moment the door closed and I was alone in a room with Hani, Waleed, Sab'r's father and his younger brother. Then the door opened again and a dozen men silently filed in, all ready to give their account of the story.

Sab'r's name means cactus, like the spiny cacti that line the dirt road leading into the village, and also someone who is patient, who can wait.

'He was like his name,' said his father, who did not cry, but looked worn and shocked. 'He was tough and hard but inside he was also kind.'

His son's brief résumé is indistinguishable from hundreds of other shabbab: born at home in Faqu'a on 29 December 1967, seven months after Israel occupied the West Bank. One of his uncles, sitting cross-legged in a corner, said that Sab'r was unlucky because he was conceived in the year of the occupation.

Sab'r went to school until grade six, an unremarkable student by all accounts, and then he went on to a technical school in Jenin. His mother said that he was quiet and respectful and they 'never had any difficulties'. He became political at the start of the intifada in 1987, on a low level at first, painting slogans and throwing stones, but he later had the grand privilege of being recruited by the Black Panthers.

With the group Sab'r grew more involved in active combat, so to speak: killing collaborators and ambushing Israeli soldiers. He gained a reputation for fearlessness, and became one of the village leaders of the intifada. His father said he was deeply religious. He was imprisoned twice, once for eighteen days, the second time for twenty-six months 'for security purposes'.

His father, like most fathers of politically active children, knew what his son was doing but never considered the fact that he might not come home some day. He was on his way to the mosque to pray at midday when he heard from a neighbour that there had been a shooting down the road and that three shabbab had been killed. It did not occur to him that it could be Sab'r, but later, while he was praying, he said that he had an odd sensation.

'More than a feeling, almost a vision, or a voice that said, "If you had to die for the cause, would you sacrifice one of your children, or give yourself?" And for some reason I immediately thought I will give a son because I have three more.' He did not think about it again until someone came to him and said that it was his son who had died. 'Then I felt ashamed, I felt wretched, I felt as though I had been hit with a bullet.'

Someone drove him to the spot where his son had been killed. At first he could only see the car the Black Panthers had been driving, shattered with bullet-holes, but when he saw the car seat splashed with blood, he knew for certain that one of the bodies that had been taken away by the Israelis was the body of his son.

The father began to cry then, quietly, and one of the older relations came and put a hand on his shoulder. 'That's enough,' he said fiercely to me, pointing to my notebook. 'No more questions.'

But the father raised his hand and said that he wanted to continue the story. Sab'r was driving a van with six of his comrades, all of them Black Panthers and all of them 'wanted men' in connection with Yoram Cohen's death in Misilliah. They had been living in caves in the hills and had come down to the village when they noticed that they were being followed by a special unit car that was filled with Israeli soldiers disguised as Palestinians. Sab'r panicked, tried to turn the van round and head back in the opposite direction towards the mountains. When they realized it was too late, that they were trapped, the six men jumped out of the van, grabbing their guns, and opened fire on the soldiers.

Sab'r stayed in the van and he was hit first: the first nine-millimetre bullet from the mini-Uzi, his father said, pierced his chest, his shoulder, his neck and his arms. His uncle interrupted the story here to say that Sab'r had also been shot in the eye and the legs. His father sat up very straight and said, 'If he felt pain, he would not have cried out.' His father believed that Sab'r probably died immediately and quietly about two kilometres from the village where he had lived all his life.

The IDF report gave a slightly different version of the death of Sab'r:

On 25 September 1991 Border Patrol and the army were on patrol at about 1.30 p.m. in the eastern quarter of Jenin when they approached a vehicle with seven Palestinians inside. The soldiers became suspicious and asked the car to stop. The driver of the car tried to run over one of the soldiers and the remaining soldiers fired at the driver and killed him. A number of men got out of the car while one held a sub-machine-gun and another a pistol. The IDF fired at them. Official military sources state that in the incident three of the passengers were killed, including the driver, one was wounded, not seriously, and was evacuated to hospital for immediate treatment. The three remaining were caught, apprehended and brought to interrogation.

The IDF office said they confiscated one pistol, one sub-machine-gun, a knife and ammunition. Curfew was imposed on the villages of Qabatia, Misilliah and the area around Faqu'a.

The father, still harbouring a faint hope that Sab'r might be one of the men who lived, went to the hospital in Jenin to try to find him. He was turned away and told to go to the police. At the police station he was questioned about Sab'r's political acti-vism and his contacts, and then told in a brutal voice, 'Your son was killed.' They said to come back the next day at 10.00 a.m. At ten o'clock the father returned and was informed by the police that they did not have the body and that he must return to the police station at two o'clock. Back at the police station he was asked to identify the body, but he must come back that evening at eleven. He returned at eleven and was sent away again.

The same thing happened the next day. On the third day he was shown into a waiting-room. After two hours he was taken in to see the body.

'Then I was told that I had to pay four hundred Israeli shekels for the ambulance and the helicopter,' the father said. 'They even charge us for the bullets that kill our children.'

When he was finally allowed to bring Sab'r's body home, his house was surrounded by the army, who feared general unrest and demonstrations. The funeral was meant to begin at 6.00 p.m., but people were prohibited from entering the village and five shabbab were beaten up. On 28 September, three days after he was killed, Sab'r was buried.

'I think he always knew he was going to die,' his father said, 'because when I asked him when he was going to get married, he always refused. He said there were more important things to do.'

We left the Beit al-'Azza and drove slowly to the place where the women were mourning. Hani came inside with me, but the other men stayed outside. The mother was beyond grief. She was sobbing wildly and shouting and when she saw me, she fled up the stairs, stumbling slightly on her long black dress. Hani called her back, soothing her in a gentle voice, and at last she came down and gave me her hand and sat down between her two daughters.

When I asked her if she felt she could have stopped Sab'r from his activities, which were dangerous, she twisted her head round and looked at me sharply. 'I could not prevent him!' she shrieked. 'Of course we feel this deep sadness, but at the same time, we are proud that we have a martyr. We thank Allah. It is all from Allah, and we have to accept that. We thank Allah that he died for Palestine and for his homeland.'

She stared at a spot above my left shoulder and began to cry. I sat rooted to my chair, not knowing what to do, until one of the sisters stood up and addressed me in English. 'I think you had better go.'

Outside Sab'r's family's house Palestinian flags were flying and the children of Faqu'a were celebrating the fact that they had another martyr in their village. There were no signs of the army at all; the streets were deserted except for the tiny children. Slogans go up on walls in bright-red paint within hours of a death or a clash with the army, and that day the children were writing about Sab'r and martyrdom: 'Let's make the intifada bigger and better' and 'Sab'r is a candle burnt to give light to the road to our independence.' A group of four or five small boys, about eight years old, surrounded my car and stared at me intently.

'Do you know who lived in that house?' I said, pointing to Sab'r's house.

Four heads nodded solemnly. One said, 'A martyr.'

Hani asked them if they knew what Sab'r did. The smallest of the group leaned over and stuck his head into my window. 'He was a Black Panther,' he breathed. 'The bravest of them all.'

Waleed's mother, who owned an all-purpose shop in the souk in Jenin, sat on a chair next to mine and dragged a comb through my matted hair. Everything I did seemed to make her laugh: the way I dressed, the way I spoke, the way I pronounced Arabic, the way I drank my mint tea without sugar. She picked up a tin of face cream and showed it to me – BENSAL: 'for all post-inflammatory infections, anti-freckles, acne, skin, wrinkles, enlarges small breasts, rough skin, dryness, eczema'. She ran her fingers across my nose as if she could feel my freckles. She spoke some English. She pointed to the jar of cream and then my nose, and grinned wildly.

Waleed burst in through the door. His right arm was in a sling, the result of a clash the night before with collaborators, he said, and he was smoking with his left hand. 'It's a fractured wrist and it's not the first time,' he said miserably. 'I write about them all the time and they come after me. Last week they threatened me with a machine-gun.'

He had a black eye and a long scratch down his cheek. He looked edgy and irritable. Why was it that I did not believe anything he said? All of his movements were jumpy. First he put a tape of Egyptian music into the recorder, then he sprayed deodorant on, pointing the can at his armpits, but spraying on the outside of his shirt. I turned my head away as the smell of the cheap deodorant permeated the small shop. He pushed me out of the way to comb his hair and stared at himself in the mirror.

'My mother likes you,' he said. 'She says you have a sense of humour.'

The mother smiled and said something in Arabic.

'She says to tell you that your life is easier than hers,' Waleed said and added, 'as if you didn't know.'

Then he turned abruptly towards me and placed my bag on my shoulder. 'Now. We go.' He grabbed some film from the shelves and stuffed it, along with a camera that was under the counter, into a striped shoulder bag he was holding. 'You carry it,' he said and tossed it to me, I suppose because I was the woman. 'He's waiting. We're late.'

We were going to see a Black Panther who was on the run for another incident, and who had spent the night in a neighbour's house in Jenin. He was waiting to see me before he left for the caves in the hills. As we drove to the house, Waleed asked if I could take him back to Jerusalem with me that night. He indicated for us to pull over at a house and dashed out of the car.

When he was out of the car, Hani looked at me carefully and spoke in English. 'You know now that Waleed is wanted and that he no longer has an identity card. Before you decide to take him to Jerusalem, you should know that.'

I said that if he did not have a card, I could not bring him in my car.

Hani was silent for a moment. 'It is your decision, but if it was me, I would do it.'

'What is he wanted for? Killing collaborators?'

Hani shrugged. 'I don't know. Don't ask him, please. Sometimes you ask things that you should not. This is something you should not ask.'

I thought about it for roughly two seconds. Jerusalem was completely sealed up with border checks because it was coming up to the first anniversary of the Temple Mount massacre, in which seventeen Palestinians were killed when the army opened fire. Jerusalem was in a state of paranoia. Palestinians were not even being allowed into the city without Israeli identity cards. I could not risk bringing Waleed, who was wanted by the army for something he would not reveal to me, in my car. I told Hani that I was sorry, but I could not. He looked at me and gave me a wry smile. 'And I thought you were one of us,' he said and turned to look out of the window.

The Black Panther, who was called Omar, was staying in a safe house that belonged to an old woman. She answered the door wearing a traditional Palestinian embroidered dress and, seeing Waleed, she took his face in both her hands and covered it in kisses. A baby was asleep in the corner and when I bent down to pick it up, the old woman took my hand and said, 'That baby is an orphan. Her mother died of a heart attack when the army raided. And I was beaten up. Imagine! An old woman!'

'How old are you?'

Her face creased. 'Seventy, maybe eighty? No, maybe seventy-two. The army won't come here now. They are afraid of me when I shout.'

The wanted man, she said softly, was in the back room. He had just woken up. She led the way through the room where the entire family slept and ate to a small window, and motioned for me to climb through. I bent down and Hani pushed me gently through to the other side, a flat roof with coffee cans filled with soil and tomato plants. Lying on his back on the mattress, smoking a cigarette, was the smiling Omar. He jumped up when he saw me and moved the two-foot sabre that was next to him on the blanket. Waleed, who followed me through the window, made the introductions and then became shy in the presence of the wanted man. Like martyrs, they have a respectability within the community and are at the top of the resistance hierarchy.

Omar was short and dark, with adolescent acne. As soon as he heard I was a journalist, he became wildly animated. He wanted his photograph taken with his face masked by his kef-fiyeh, brandishing his sabre above his head, standing on the rooftops. He wanted to show me how he ran away if he heard a knock on the door (by leaping up on the roof and across to the house next door, then down into an alley into another safe house). He wanted to show me how he slept with his trainers on, ready to sprint away from the enemy. He wanted to tell me every detail of his life – what he ate and how he slept four hours a night.

He wanted to show me his bullet wounds, his scars from battle and his broken tooth from getting beaten up by soldiers in Jenin prison. He said he was twenty-three, had been a Black Panther since 1988, had been on the run for two years, had not seen his mother for forty days and he was indeed prepared to die at any given moment.

'Are you afraid?' I said.

Omar made a clucking noise with his tongue. Waleed and Hani shook their heads. 'I don't feel any fear. This is daily life for us. I always expect them to come and get me and I am ready. Even when you wait this long, you are always ready. I know I will be caught. I have to do my best until then.'

'And to die?'

'It is what I hope.'

The old woman came outside on the terrace to pick herbs that were growing in small tubs on the roof. 'Yes, he expects to die, but only for his homeland!' she shouted.

'I prefer victory or death,' Omar added dramatically.

The old woman brought mint tea. I asked Omar what his work with the Black Panthers consisted of. He listed his duties casually, looking bored. 'Increasing activity. Encouraging people. Killing soldiers when we can get them,' he said, without missing a beat.

'And do you ever think that a soldier is a human being and has a wife or a baby?'

He grew defensive. 'Why do I have to think about a soldier with a baby? Maybe he should think twice before he comes to the occupied territories and kills women and babies and beats shabbab.'

'Where do you get your guns?'

'Some people get them from soldiers. They trade them for drugs that the Palestinians get from Lebanon.'

I must have looked sceptical, because he suddenly jumped to his feet and began to pace around the small rooftop. 'You think I am lying?' he shouted. 'Look. As Palestinians we always wanted the peace, but this is the only way.' He sat down and shook his head wildly.

'Omar is also a very good singer,' Waleed said in a soothing voice, trying to break the drama of the moment. 'At demonstrations he is always the one with the microphone. Isn't that right, Omar?'

Omar sat in the corner looking petulant. Hani nudged me. 'Ask him to sing for us.'

'You ask him to sing,' I said. I had had enough of the wanted man.

Omar needed little urging. He stood up, clasped his hands behind his back and tilted his head. He began to sing in a terrible, out-of-tune voice.

> 'Our homeland's name is Palestine
> On Jerusalem it is written.
> Since we were born
> Palestine has been under a holocaust
> Called the nakbeh, the disaster.
> In all our towns and villages,
> In Beit Sahour, in Bethlehem, in Beit Jala,
> The heroes' land is our example.
> In Kufor, Malek, Jenin,
> We will raise the Arab flag.'

He finished and turned to me. 'You tell James Baker that our homeland cannot stay occupied.'

Then Omar became even more lively. He grasped Waleed's camera and asked him to take photographs of him with me, because I was 'from England'. I refused. Hani looked at me disapprovingly.

'It's not so much to ask. Just take a photograph for me to keep.'

I made a feeble excuse, but as I bent my head to write in my notebook, Omar sat next to me on one side and Hani on the other, and Waleed began to snap. I kept my head down while the men smiled broadly as though they were posing for a photograph on holiday. Then Waleed and Hani switched places and I pretended to reach into my bag so that my head got cut out of the picture.

They were actually enjoying this, I thought. How is it that an activist can be so stupid as to think that someone, like the Shin Bet, will not find their photographs after they are captured? The answer is simple: because they never think they will be captured.

I did not speak for a while. I was thinking about the risks that people like the wanted man took, that someone like Waleed, even Hani, took. Risks that seemed purely stupid to me. Later Hani asked me gently, 'Why are you angry with me?'

I wanted to say, 'Because you treat this like some kind of war game, like kids playing with toy guns, but this is real and people are getting hurt.' But in the end I decided to say nothing. 'I'm not angry.'

He smiled with a kind of innocent relief.

A few days afterwards Omar was caught by the army. Waleed gave me the photographs 'to take back to England'. All I could see was the grinning wanted man brandishing a sword over his head, his trainers untied, his face frozen in an arrogant grin.

The two other Black Panthers who had been killed on the road outside Faqu'a came from Qabatia, another village outside Jenin, and that week a mass funeral was to be held for both of them. The IDF had imposed a curfew on the village after the killings and I had to wait two days before I could get inside. Even Waleed, who claimed he was afraid of no man, refused to bring me to Qabatia while it was still under curfew. Qabatia, he said in a shaky voice, was too hot. In the past few months eight collaborators had been killed. What made someone become a collaborator? Waleed had an easy answer. He said that a Palestinian became a collaborator because he or she had a weak soul. 'Either that or the Israelis harass them and make them afraid when they are arrested, so they decide to do it. Sometimes they have no choice.'

'But you have a choice when you kill them, don't you?'

Waleed shrugged. Palestinians hate talking about collaborators. It is the dark spot on their great and glorious cause.

As we waited for a ride to Qabatia, we were sitting in Waleed's mother's house in a room dominated by a red banner that read 'The Communist Party, 1919–1989'. Waleed's younger sister, who was about my age, came into the room and asked for a cigarette. Waleed refused, stood up and in an angry voice told her to leave us alone. The sister looked stricken.

'Why can't she stay?' I asked.

'Because she's a girl,' he said sheepishly.

I said I was a girl too, and Waleed blushed. 'But you're not a Muslim.'

He changed the subject quickly and said he wanted to talk about Qabatia, where the resistance movement against the Israel occupation was very strong. One of the dead Black Panther's uncles, who was visiting Waleed, proudly informed me that during the 1967 war Yasser Arafat had come to Qabatia to organize an underground movement and in 1970 seventy-eight men were arrested at one time by the Israelis.

The Black Panther, Hassan Ahed Alawny Kimed, was twenty years old when he died in the ambush, the third oldest in a family of eight. His father, a friend of Waleed, entered the room at that moment looking unshaven and tired, but remarkably steady given the fact that his son had been killed a few days before. He shook my hand and reached into his wallet to produce a snapshot of his son holding a gun in one hand and a machete in the other, standing in front of an elaborate picture of Fatah, and urged me to keep it. I slipped it between the pages of my notebook, making a mental note to destroy it before I left Israel. There was another one too, of a collage that Fatah had made after Hassan died; he said he would show it to me, but he wanted to keep it for himself. He did not mind telling me about his son because he was proud of him, he said. He had died 'resisting the occupation'.

As he spoke, he toyed with the identity card that poked out of his shirt pocket. He was wearing the Palestinian uniform of grey polyester trousers and a blue button-down shirt, but on his feet were stylish hiking boots like those I have seen teenagers wearing on the streets of Rome. It was a strange juxtaposition. I remember staring at those boots and wondering where could he have got them from in Jenin.

He told me that his family had been in Qabatia since 'my grandfather's grandfather's grandfather. The Jews were a minority then, only five per cent of the population, but we lived side by side. Most of the land was farmed; there were no cars, only donkeys and carts. The land was so peaceful and so simple. I remember the quiet of the hillsides when I was a boy. Palestine was so beautiful.'

One of Hassan's uncles said he was a 'historian of sorts'. I asked him if he could recall 1948, after the Israeli War of Independence carved up the state of Palestine, the time that the Palestinians refer to as their holocaust. I asked him to think back to before the Israelis occupied the land and further back before the Jordanians, who were the occupiers from 1948 to 1967. The uncle scratched his head and asked me how much I knew about the Palestinians. A bit, I told him.

'Then I will give you a history lesson. The Palestinians have been here for many thousands and thousands of years. The first people who lived on this land were Canaanites and they were our grandfathers. The Palestinians came from near Greece and occupied Palestine. Then the Jews came from Sinai and settled in a part of Palestine. Those are historic facts. We are the Jews' cousins. From the same family tree. We don't hate the Jews for their religion. We lived together in the past and we can live together in the future.'

'But,' I said, 'there was a time when the PLO said they wanted to throw all the Jews into the sea.'

There was a brief scuffle of feet. The uncle cleared his throat. 'In Fatah we no longer say that we want to throw the Jews into the sea. When I dream of Palestine now, I dream of two nations living together, a peaceful nation. A beautiful nation.'

To emphasize his point he quoted a Palestinian proverb: 'The night does not stay the night and the day does not stay the day.'

Hassan's father explained. 'It means that we are now during the night, but the day must come.' He sipped his coffee. 'Israel is supported by America but not always.'

Hassan's cousin, who had been sitting quietly in a corner for most of the conversation, turned to me. 'What do you want most from life?'

'I don't know. I suppose to be happy.'

'Happy! What is happy? All I want is to get rid of this green identity card which says I've been in prison and am forbidden to enter Israel. I want just once to drive down the road and not to have to produce it for some soldier to check. That's all I want.'

'Tell me about your son,' I said, wondering when a child develops a sense of violence. When does he become capable of pulling a trigger and ending a life, or when does he lose the fear that his life may end? Hassan's father could not answer that question, but he could tell me about his son. As a child Hassan used to carve pistols from wood and play Arabs and Jews instead of cowboys and Indians with his friends. He was not terribly clever, but he had a fine sense of humour and was good at sports. He got as far as the sixth grade and then he went to vocational school in Nablus, where he learned how to become a machinist. His uncle said he was best at playing football, because he had a strong throwing arm. Later on in life, when he was not involved in collaborator killings or ambushes, he still liked to play football.

Hassan's political awakening came early. As a small boy he

would sit and watch while the Israeli soldiers raided the village, and he told his mother that it made him sick to see them and he wanted revenge. She would hold him and caution patience, but she remembered the rage that the tiny child felt. When the intifada began, he joined the local boys and threw stones, stacked tyres in the middle of the road and burnt them and learned how to make a Molotov. At first he was working with local Fatah committees, but later, after he was shot by the army during a clash, he decided to seek out the Black Panthers.

When Hassan was shot with a dumdum bullet in 1990, he lay on his back in hospital for nearly three weeks with a scar ten inches long that seared his abdomen. He hated being in bed, his brother said, hated the helplessness and the immobility, 'because there were a lot of demonstrations at that time and he couldn't go. He couldn't even walk, so we carried him to the window to watch.' For three months he was in agony, his gut twisted in what seemed like an endless spasm. After one month he forced himself to take a few steps and started to regain his strength. After eight months he had a second operation to remove pieces of shrapnel.

Later his friends noticed the change in Hassan, the added determination and the zeal that he put into his activities. He became a Black Panther and he said he had resolved to fight the occupation with guns.

'He was convinced that the only way to get rid of the Israelis was through an armed struggle,' said his brother.

Hassan had been a wanted man for six months before he died. He and his six comrades had been living in the caves near Faqu'a for about five days when they decided to change their position for security purposes. Hassan's uncle claimed someone had warned the Black Panthers that the Israelis wanted them badly. Shortly before the ambush an unknown car came into the village with Shin Bet officers dressed as Palestinians pretending to sell carpets. 'And they were asking about the boys, but everyone knew they were Jews. They moved in a suspicious way.'

They believed it was the same unit that killed Hassan shortly afterwards, when the blue Volkswagen van was ambushed.

'When I found out he was dead,' the father said calmly, stirring three teaspoons of sugar into his coffee, 'we were asked by the civil administration to go to identify the body. The government man came out and said to me, "We killed your son." And I looked him in the eyes and said, "You killed one. But even if you killed five of my children, I still have three more. That's how I feel."'

The Israeli army officer turned to him and said, 'I'm a father too. Don't you care that we killed your son?'

Hassan's father replied, 'I am a father, and yes, I have emotions, but our religion teaches us to die for our homeland.'

The Israeli was stunned and looked down at his notebook. He said that he would return the body on condition that Hassan's father promised him there would be no demonstrations at the funeral.

'I told him that it was not my responsibility.'

A *khamsin*, a hot, dry wind, was blowing through Qabatia when I arrived in the village to go to the Beit al-'Azza of the two martyrs. Before I got out of the car with Waleed and Hani, I adjusted my headscarf so that none of my hair was showing.

'You look like a good Muslim wife,' Hani said approvingly.

Waleed glanced down the deserted street and nodded for us to enter a door on the right, leading into a courtyard where the mosque stood. I had decided, since the incident of the photographs with Omar, that I did not like Waleed or his flighty manner. Something about him set me on edge – the way that he pronounced my name in the Arabic fashion, the way that he dictated what I wrote down, the way he pummelled me with propaganda. When I did not do what he wanted, he would say, 'You are not with us.' There was no point in telling him that no, I was not meant to be with them.

I ducked down low beneath the arched doorway and entered the dusty courtyard where the wake was being held. In the sunlight I blinked rapidly: there were about two hundred men gathered inside the enclosed walls and about ten Israeli soldiers in full riot gear stalking the area.

'How many people would you say are here?' I asked Waleed.

'At least five hundred,' he answered, loading film into his cheap camera. He was looking at the soldiers and twitching with nervous energy.

'There's going to be a clash,' I said to Hani.

'Probably,' he answered offhandedly.

A soldier, patrolling the area near the mosque, spotted me and stopped dead in his tracks. I saw him turn to tell his companion that I was there. Hani saw it too. He grabbed my arm roughly and pulled me into a small one-roomed house where eight men stood in a circle, in the middle of which was a huge brass tray piled with food. Someone gave me a chair, someone else poured me another tiny cup of coffee. Then I was surrounded.

'Sahafia! From England! Her name is Jenin! Arabic name!'

'You are from England?'

'What does your government think of the intifada?'

'Are the English with us?'

'Are you with us?'

'She is with us.'

'Do you know George Bush?'

I was clenching and unclenching my fists because I was having a bout of intense claustrophobia: the small, airless room filled with cigarette smoke, the men circling me, pulling at my sleeve to get my attention, the tenth cup of black coffee that day. I had a headache; I wanted to go outside, but the soldiers were nearby and I could not. One man pulled at my sleeve and I abruptly yanked myself free and sat slightly apart. The tension in the room – because the army was outside and a clash seemed imminent – was fierce. Hani stood next to me.

'Relax,' he said quietly. 'You must be strong. See, they are not afraid and they are Palestinians. They are in danger, not you. You have a press card, a passport. You are protected.'

Outside, the confrontation had begun and there was the sound of shouting. I looked out of the window to see the soldiers charging into one of the houses and dragging out two shabbab. I saw Hassan's father standing quietly on the side, watching, and I remembered him saying it was not his responsibility. A soldier raised his gun in the air.

'Tear-gas canister,' Hani said.

Waleed danced in and out of the hut, his slim body a live wire of tense energy. He was taking photographs, then throwing the used film rolls in my handbag. 'You hold it. They cannot touch you.'

Men gathered at the window to watch the scene outside. Waleed grabbed my bag from my shoulder and then, for a reason I have never quite understood, yanked my passport out of my bag. I snatched it back from him.

'No,' I said.

His face dropped. 'You are not with us?'

There was a shout. Waleed! Someone dragged him outside. His camera was stuffed in my bag. Hani grabbed me and pushed me towards the window. More cigarettes were lit, the room was so smoky it was difficult to see. There was the constant sound of snorting and some of the men spat on the floor. Then there was an argument over the film, and someone reached into my bag to remove the rolls of film.

'I don't want my face in that film!' shouted one of the men.

'I could not agree with you more,' I said. I turned round to Hani and said, 'I'm going.'

He pleaded with me: 'Stay.'

'You stay. I'm going.' I told him I wanted to see the martyr's mother.

I could see in his eyes that Hani knew I was leaving so that I would not be tear-gassed with the men, and he was hurt. 'If I am willing to be tear-gassed, then why not you?'

He encouraged me to talk to Hassan's brother first and, grudgingly, because I felt I had enough about Hassan and I did not really wish to write about him any more, I took out my notebook. Hassan's older brother was eager to talk, and as the brother of a martyr he commanded a certain amount of respect. He watched me as I flipped open my book and uncapped my pen.

'Write this,' he said, pointing at the blank page.

I wrote down the words. 'Hot. Overpowering. Propaganda.' Hassan's brother smiled. He thought I was writing about him.

Hassan's brother said he heard about Hassan's death the day after he died, while listening to a radio broadcast from Cyprus. 'At that moment I could not think. I only wanted to go to the village and to see what had happened to my brother. When I got home, my mother was crying. She said we have to be proud, you have to raise your head high.'

Someone brought in more coffee and cartons of cigarettes. I waved both away and directed Hassan's brother to continue.

'I can't describe the feeling. The feeling of any mother who loses a son. And I know my mother, and I know that if she could, she would have given her own life for her son. But she was still proud.'

I was wondering if his brother's life was worth trading. He seemed to sense this.

'If we want a state,' he said, 'we have to be ready to give our lives for it. We don't even think twice about it.'

I wandered out of the hut, out of the madness of the stinking courtyard and the Beit al-'Azza, and into the village to find Hassan's mother. She was in a big house at the edge of a field, surrounded by women dressed from head to toe in black. She looked haggard. She was forty-five years old. She was not crying.

'No, I feel happy with Allah,' she said, clutching her breast. 'Even now I don't cry because Allah is taking care of him.'

Your son, I asked myself, but could not possibly argue. Exhausted, I found the car outside the courtyard and drove back to Jenin.

A meeting had been arranged with wanted men in another village outside Jenin, an ancient village called 'Arrabeh. Twice I went to the designated safe house and twice I missed the shabbab by five minutes because the army had come and they had fled. Wanted men, I was told, do not stay in one place for very long. We had left Waleed with his mother in Jenin and met up with two more Palestinian sources. Hani had made me promise not to mention Waleed's name to them, but would not tell me why.

'Something to do with loyalties,' he muttered.

One of the new sources was small and wiry and grinned inanely all the time. He had recently become engaged and wanted money to bring me to the Black Panthers in 'Arrabeh. The other was tall and brooding with a thick moustache. His name was Muhammed, and he was looking for a wife.

'You see, he even has a house built for the right girl,' said Hussein, the small one. 'Maybe you could be that girl?'

'No. I'm not Muslim.'

Hussein translated this for Muhammed, who answered in

Arabic. Hussein said to me. 'Not a problem. He said you can convert. And your name is Arabic. This is a start.' It became a running joke for the next three days.

Waiting for the wanted men was unnerving. We sat in the spacious two-storeyed house that Muhammed had built for the mythical wife, eating green grapes and drinking tap water. Hani and Hussein taught me Arabic phrases. 'Give me the plate, please.' 'How about some water?' 'May I use the lavatory?' 'Ya'allah habibi!' – Let's go, my dear! Muhammed was restless and pacing because he had arranged the meeting. Every few minutes he got up and checked the window or went outside and sat on the step. His mother, who lived downstairs with his sisters, was making soap from olive oil and had spread the green mixture in a giant vat on the grass in front of the house. There was the faint smell of fruit trees from an orchard in the distance.

Muhammed sat on the stairs and spat grape seeds on to the grass. He decided that we should go to every safe house in 'Arrabeh and look for the shabbab. I climbed into the driver's seat and Muhammed put out a warning hand: either he would not drive with me, or I was too conspicuous as a driver. I shrugged and handed the keys to Hani.

We drove for two hours through the village and into the next village, looking for the boys, asking locals who could be trusted.

'Wayn-l-shabbab?' – Where are the boys?

'They've gone back to the hills,' sighed Hani. 'It's your fault. You are always late.'

I said that we would find them and Hani looked at me dubiously. There was silence in the car as we drove up a winding hill and turned into the village square. Then Hani slammed on the brakes. I pitched forward.

'What are you doing?' Hussein shouted from the back seat.

I looked up. Halting my useless Fiat Uno were about fifteen

mulathameen, their faces hidden behind elaborately wrapped red silk masks, with slashes cut out for their eyes and mouths. All of them brandished hatchets, and one, who looked about sixteen, blocked my car by laying his hatchet down on the bonnet. He checked the car and I could see the surprise in his eyes behind the silk mask when he saw me, a western woman with a pony-tail, crammed into a car with four Palestinians.

These mulathameen were members of the DFLP (Democratic Front for the Liberation of Palestine) and they usually carried out their work at night. There was something eerie and menacing about seeing them working in the daylight, in their jeans and trainers and masks. I scanned the faces of the people who had been walking through the square and had been stopped: most of them were staring solemnly at the mulathameen, but others were impatient, or agitated. Two young women, dressed in knee-length dresses and headscarves, were wheeling a Baby Buggy and giggling at them. The young boys were standing near them, mouths open in admiration. After a few minutes of keeping us waiting one of the leaders stood on top of another stalled car's hood, grabbed a microphone and began to deliver his speech.

'The Democratic Front is the only leadership of the intifada!' he screeched. 'There is only one leader and one leader only.'

'That's Omar up there,' I said, trying to joke, 'with the bullhorn.'

'Who's Omar?' Hussein asked.

'We met him the other day, with Waleed. Remember he sang? With the awful voice?'

Hani shot me a dark look. I had forgotten that I was not meant to mention Waleed, or my trip to see Omar. Rival PLO factions.

Hussein was not listening. He was watching the mulathameen with great interest. 'And here is a warning to heed strike days,' he translated. 'And here is a warning to boycott Israeli goods. Ah, here is the good part: a warning to collaborators that they will be killed for working with informers. They will be killed without warning.'

The mulathameen's voice took on a hysterical edge. 'The intifada is the struggle of the Palestinian people! We will regain our homeland!'

He brought his hatchet down. We were allowed to pass. Hani drove slowly, slightly shakily, outside the square. The mulathameen seemed to have disappeared. Blocking the square was a boy of about twelve with enormous ears, which stuck out, and red hair. I noticed him because of his hair. I looked at him and he looked at me.

We drove back to Muhammed's house and sat outside until the sun sank into the hills, waiting for the three Black Panthers to turn up.

The *adan*, the call for prayer, had already begun. Muhammed talked about the men we were waiting for. He said they were 'very important, very high up and very wanted', and the ground rules were laid for my meeting: do not ask their names, do not ask their activities and do not ask any specifics about their organization.

'Do you agree?'

I nodded.

We ate food provided by Muhammed's mother, who came out of the kitchen with a battered tray covered with tiny dishes. She set it down, arranged the dishes in a neat circle and quickly scurried back into the kitchen, where she watched us eat from a window in the door. There were courgettes stuffed with meat covered in a milky sauce; mashed aubergines; soft cheese and pitta bread, olives, hummus. Hussein speared a courgette and said, chewing with his mouth open, 'You must learn to cook like this if you want to be married to an Arab.'

Muhammed looked faintly irritated.

The men ate, stopping for cigarettes in between courses, and then moved to the overstuffed sofas where they ate grapes and drank black coffee. Muhammed poured thick orange soda into glasses, and we sat in silence for a few minutes before we heard a sharp whistle outside the door. Hussein tensed and jumped to his feet. There was a quick knock, another whistle, and the Black Panthers chose that moment to storm in, wielding guns and cigarettes with equal ease.

There were three of them, and they all looked tired and very old, though later I found out that none of them was older than twenty-two. They were not masked. Following them was the red-haired twelve-year-old whom I instantly recognized from the village square earlier that day.

The Panthers ignored me for the moment, motioning to the men to sit down. Then they checked the doors and windows, the couches and chairs and, satisfied that they were in a safe place, directed me with their guns to take a seat opposite them.

They placed their guns – one magnum, two pistols – across their knees and stared at me politely. One asked if everyone in England had hair the same colour as mine.

They laughed. They each had a sense of humour, and I began to relax. The twelve-year-old bodyguard went outside and said he would whistle if there was any trouble.

One of the Panthers came over and handed me a cigarette, a Farid. I did not want it, but I thought it might be wise to take it, and as he lit it, he noticed that my hand shook slightly. He asked me if I was afraid of him.

'Not you,' I said, and pointed to his gun. 'It's your gun that I don't like.'

All three made clucking noises with their tongues. Fear, they said, was an emotion that they simply did not understand. They knew they could be killed at any moment, and it was the choice that they made. If they died, they would go straight to Allah. It was what they hoped for. Allahu Akbah. God is great.

'So, please do not fear the gun,' said one, who had blue eyes and a chiselled face. 'The gun is our salvation.'

There was a knock on the door and all three jumped to attention, their guns ready. They relaxed when they saw that it was only Muhammed's mother, who brought in tea and small almond biscuits. If she saw the guns, or noticed anything unusual about the dishevelled Black Panthers, she gave no indication. She poured the tea and offered the Panthers a biscuit. She pointed to the sugar. The Panthers crammed the biscuits into their mouths and said that they had been on the run, sleeping in the mountains and hiding from the army, for the past two years. These last two months, one complained, had been especially trying because of their increased activities.

What activities, I asked. Hani, next to me, groaned.

Resisting the occupation, I was told.

In what way, I pressed. Killing collaborators?

The one with the blue eyes became the designated speaker. 'Listen to me,' he said, chewing the biscuit with his mouth open. 'The Palestinians under the intifada have to face two facts. Either to be martyred or to go to this university called prison. At the beginning of the intifada we threw stones, and had a few M-16s. Now, times are different. We have Uzis, Kalashnikovs, machine-guns, knives, home-made bombs, swords. Most of us have knives, all of us have guns.'

Where do you get them?

Hani stiffened.

'From dead collaborators. Through gun dealers inside Israel. Through our organization. And from Israeli soldiers. We trade for drugs.' He made a loud sniffing gesture on the back of his hand. Cocaine, he said, from Lebanon.

Another Panther, wearing a black Reebok T-shirt, said that he would give me The Facts About The Black Panthers. They were formed at the beginning of the intifada and membership was a bestowed and sacred honour: 'So many of the shabbab would like to join us, but they can't. Only the best can, because we are the military and security branch of our organization. The only way you can join is when someone gets arrested or killed, and then there is a place open.'

They operate secretly from the villages, doing their work by night or wearing masks in the day. No one is supposed to know who they are or how they work. No one knows where their guerrilla camp in the mountains is, except their guards.

Interesting fact: they claim to sleep on sleeping-bags donated by the Israeli Peace Movement. When I expressed disbelief, they reassured me: 'And we have been visited by members of the Knesset, who came to show solidarity.'

The smallest Panther stood up and began pacing. He said that he wanted to tell his story. 'I was born in 1970, under the occupation. All my life, I knew nothing but life under the Israeli army. My eyes became opened when I saw the Jewish terrorists against my people. And because of that, and because of watching the harassment, day after day, I knew that I had two roads to choose: one to do nothing, the other to take the road to the revolution.' Having said his bit, he sat down heavily.

The one with the black T-shirt cleared his throat. His story, he said, was different. He was twenty years old, ten years younger than me, and looked about forty. 'I did not really choose this path myself. Both my brothers were in prison and were always after me to be more active politically, to do more for the cause. When I was fourteen, I was imprisoned for eleven days, inter-rogated and tortured. The Israelis put me, naked, in a cactus plant in the rain for two days. They put me in the "banana" position and beat me with clubs and with their feet. The next time they arrested me I was fifteen. I was in prison for three months.' He stopped. I knew that something terrible had happened to him; later Hani told me they had given him electric shocks on his genitals.

The third one, with the blue eyes, who was nineteen, said, 'We have decided that we can gain our freedom and independence only by using weapons.'

I asked each of them if they had ever killed anyone. All three nodded. I asked if they had had any remorse when they killed someone, at the actual moment that they pulled the trigger. There was a silence. They asked me to repeat the question, and when they understood the meaning, they looked at me as though I were mad. 'Remorse?' asked the one with the black T-shirt incredulously.

Suddenly the room was plunged into darkness and chaos erupted. The men jumped to their feet and ran for the door, guns in hand. I stayed behind with the mother. The twelve-year-old bodyguard, who was clearly not as tough as he thought he was, ran inside stuttering. He was smacked on the head and told to be quiet.

'The army?' I asked Hani.

'No, the generator. It happens all the time in the villages.'

We went outside. The entire village was dark and peaceful. The Black Panthers flicked their lighters to continue the interview.

I asked the boy how he had joined the group. 'Through friendship and trust,' he said proudly.

'Why aren't you in school?'

'I work as a mechanic. And there are more important things than school, such as the liberation of Palestine.'

I asked him if he wanted to grow up, live a normal life, get married.

He snorted. The Black Panthers watched him carefully. 'Wanted men get married sometimes. I would like to have sons to carry on the struggle against Israel.'

There was another whistle from further on, in the brush, and another bodyguard, this one a grown-up, joined us. He was cradling his machine-gun like a baby and his cigarette glowed orange in the dark. He gestured towards the Panthers. 'Ya'allah shabbab,' he said. Let's go, guys.

One of them turned to me: 'You know George Bush?'

'Not personally,' I said.

'Take this message to him. The Palestinian people are struggling, yet we want peace. But we have the olive branch in one hand and a stone or a machine-gun in the other. It means we have to fight, but at the same time we want peace.'

The twelve-year-old grabbed my arm and pointed to another Panther: 'He says he wants to kill George Bush with his bare hands!'

The Panther shrugged.

They began to prepare to go, with an elaborate discussion of which route to take to the hills to avoid the army. Then one paused. 'Wait! You know what Bingo means?'

Bingo? 'Bingo is a game,' I said. 'The object is to pick off as many numbers as you can by the end of the game. Then you call out, "Bingo!"'

He looked satisfied. 'Because that is what the army always says when they catch or kill one of us. They say, "BINGO!"'

He stuck his fingers in his mouth and whistled sharply. The three of them, with the twelve-year-old for protection, disappeared into the darkness and then into the mountains.

I wanted to talk to the Israeli Defence Force about the Black Panthers, but I did not seem to have much luck in pinning them down with a specific answer. One soldier I met, who had served in Gaza, said, 'Black Panthers! You can call them the Sweet Rose of Texas and it's still the same. Just a bunch of crazy kids playing with guns.'

'No threat?'

'Of course they're not a threat,' he replied.

The IDF spokesman in Jerusalem acknowledged that there was such a thing as the Black Panthers and the Red Eagles, but showed the same kind of nonchalance. 'It's clear there has been a reduction in stone throwing, coupled with a sharp rise in explosives and hand grenades, as well as firing at the IDF,' he said. 'It's the use of arms that characterizes the intifada today. But from our point of view, the masked gangs are not the same as children throwing rocks, the classic face of the intifada. These *Re'ulei Panim* [masked youths] are a different category.' He paused. 'They are classic terrorists.'

He could not give a figure for how many Black Panthers were operating in the West Bank and Gaza, or how many weapons were in use. He said that in 1990 'dozens' had been arrested, but could not be more precise. He did not know the number of Red Eagles, the armed gang that pledges allegiance to the Popular Front of the Liberation of Palestine, another PLO faction. 'That,' he said ominously, 'is in the hands of the Shin Bet.'

Everyone knows the Shin Bet do not give information to the press.

I drove to the Jordanian border with a 24-year-old IDF sergeant called Michael to observe 'infiltration techniques'. I did not care about infiltration techniques, land-mines, sweeping devices or the smallest stretch of water between Jordan and Israel. I wanted to hear about the Black Panthers.

'What about them?' Michael said flippantly, his hand resting on his gun. 'A bunch of worthless kids.'

If they were so worthless, why were they in the hands of the Shin Bet?

Michael said, 'Who knows? The military moves in mysterious ways. There's no big deal with these Black Panthers. They're just fucking crazy kids who don't give a damn about their lives. Do you understand me?' He tapped his forehead. 'They are fucking crazy.' He was irritated. 'I don't want to talk to you any more about this.'

At the turn-off to the Dead Sea and Jericho we met a reserve unit and I left Michael with my car and climbed into the IDF jeep to drive to some inspection site. Inside the jeep was a young soldier who was born in Canada and spoke good English. On his wrist was a leather bracelet stamped with the words, 'THIS IS THE MANACLE'.

He had served in the occupied territories, and he was sensitive. He said he hated the feeling of being in a place where he knew that he was hated, where he knew that he was not wanted, where he knew that the people would like to kill him just because he was a Jew and not one of them.

I told him I knew what he meant. I was thinking about being in Rafah and how I had felt the hatred just because I might be a Jew.

He looked up at me and his face did not seem so young all of a sudden. 'No, you don't,' he said. 'You never will. You don't live here.'

I picked Hani up early in the morning in front of a sweet shop in Sheikh Jarrah, in Arab East Jerusalem, to drive back to Jenin. I bought a Coke in the shop and the owner presented me with a bag of boiled sweets 'because you look like such a nice girl'.

'No, really,' I said, embarrassed. He pushed them at me. 'Go. Take them.' He smiled and went back to his newspapers.

I got to the car with the sweets and paused. In the car was Hani, but there, in the back seat, was Waleed, looking dishevelled and disorientated. His arm was still in a sling. He smiled wanly, but I said nothing. He must have known I found him annoying, for he balled up his striped shoulder bag into a pillow and fell asleep.

We drove back through the hills to Jenin, a two-hour journey. Hani and Waleed slept, jerking their heads up as I went through checkpoints. I listened to Egyptian music on Jordanian radio and thought about how closely linked life and death are in Jenin.

There had been another killing that day, in the most beautiful village that I have seen in the West Bank, a horrible case of mistaken identity. I met the woman whose brother had been killed. The Israeli special unit had entered the village and thought that the victim, Emad Adik, was a wanted man they had been tracking for several days. They followed his car and sprayed it with bullets until he crashed into an electric pole, which split in two. A few hours later, when we arrived, his blood was still on the ground, the empty bullet shells scattered on the dirt. A small child took my hand and led me into the home of a woman who lived across the road and had watched the incident: warily she showed me the wayward bullet-holes that had splintered her wardrobe, the gunpowder all over her clothes. 'Thank God I was upstairs when it happened.' She bolted the door after I left.

Emad Adik was a cousin of the wanted man, a Black Panther called Nabeel Adik, who also lived in the village, and had given him a lift earlier that morning. The Israelis really wanted Nabeel, and believed they had got him: later that day, when we listened to Israeli radio, we heard them announce that they had killed Nabeel Adik.

By some freak chance I found the real wanted man, who was waiting in his home on the edge of the village with his gun.

Friends brought me to him, and I knew who he was the minute I laid eyes on him. He appeared to me to be quite mad. When I asked him if he was frightened that the Israelis would soon realize their mistake and come after him, he began to wave his gun wildly in the air. 'Let the bullets speak for themselves!' He showed little grief for the innocent cousin who had been in the wrong place at the wrong time. There was little room in his life for grief. He was, he said, too busy surviving.

But the dead man's sister was grieving; in fact, she was beyond grief. She had lost both her parents in a car crash four years ago. Emad, she insisted, was not political, was not a Black Panther, did not even belong to Fatah. He was a 24-year-old machinist, and the person she was closest to in the world.

She did not talk about Allah, or God's will, or being strong or dying for Palestine. We sat on chairs in an olive grove and she cried so hard and for so long that I thought she would be sick. Then she looked up at me and smiled slightly, as though she had forgotten I was there. 'I'm so sorry,' I said, not knowing what else to say. 'I'm sorry.'

She reached out and touched my hand, and it moved me far more than any Beit al-'Azza. 'Never mind,' she said. 'This is our life.'

Hani and I got a flat tyre late that night on the way to Ramallah and there was no jack in the boot of the car to change it. We were cold and tired and frustrated, and we pulled over to the side of the dark road and sat, sharing a cigarette, waiting for a car to pass. In the darkness I watched Hani's face and thought how different his life was from mine.

Every time a car approached I stood up and tried to flag it down. Three times a car with Jewish settlers slowed down when they saw me waving, but when they got close enough to see my blue licence plates, they quickly moved on. Finally a service taxi with eight Palestinian workers on their way home from Tel Aviv pulled over. All of the men got out and, with one steady motion, lifted the car and set the new tyre underneath. I sat on a rock and watched them; they would not let me help. After they finished, they would not take money, only my thanks, and left.

When we got to Ramallah, the border police stopped our car. It was the day before the first anniversary of the Temple Mount massacre, and everyone was anticipating some kind of retribution. We slowed down. A few seconds before he opened the window Hani said, 'OK, you are my friend and you were at my house for dinner in Ramallah. Now I am taking you home. All right?' I nodded. The soldier held out his hand, spoke to me in English. I produced my passport, Hani his blue identity card, which showed he had been born in Israel. The soldier said, 'Thank you, have a nice evening', and waved us through.

Later on, after I had dropped Hani off at his family's house in Ramallah, I drove back to Jerusalem in silence, with the radio off. As I parked the car in Yemin Moshe in Jewish West Jerusalem, I noticed that Waleed had left his striped bag behind. On impulse, I reached back and shook it open. Inside were an apple, a pen, a notebook and an elaborate dagger with a seven-inch blade.

For a second I just stared at the dagger and held it very carefully, turning it over to catch the light in the car, and then the day's events flashed through my mind: I thought of the sister in the olive grove, crying and talking about how her brother taught her how to climb a tree; and the wanted man, the one they meant to kill, waving his gun in the air and saying, 'Let the bullets speak for themselves!' and the wasted lives. Then I thought of Waleed and his insistent 'Are you with us?' and driving unsuspectingly through the border checks with Hani and the knife.

The next day I saw Hani and silently gave him the striped bag with the knife. He said not to overreact, that it was probably used to open letters. But he could not quite disguise the irritated expression on his face.

3. Defending the Enemy
The Embattled Case of Felicia Langer

Attorney Felicia Langer, who last defended draft-refuser Giora Neumann, yesterday called police to her Jerusalem office in the wake of a telephone bomb threat.

Mrs Langer told the police that the anonymous woman caller had threatened the bomb was set to go off at any minute. Police found nothing in the office, which is located on Rehov Korresh.

Jerusalem Post, 8 August 1972

Three men suspected of making a din outside the home of Felicia Langer, a Ramat Gan lawyer, were arrested by police yesterday. Mrs Langer has often represented Arabs in security cases.

Jerusalem Post, 14 June 1974

Jerusalem police last night said they were investigating the source of a cable in which the signatories – TNT or Terror Against Terror – threatened lawyer Felicia Langer.

'Thus shall all your enemies perish, O Israel,' said the cable to the defence of several Arab security cases. The cable, filed at the Jerusalem post office, was paid for by a man who gave an Ashqelon address.

Jerusalem Post, 20 June 1980

> Vandals recently spray-painted Jerusalem lawyer Feli-
> cia Langer's office door, defacing it with death threats
> and accusing her of being a PLO supporter ...
> [Langer] noted that, although this is not the first time
> she has been vilified for defending Arabs, she has never
> before been so brazenly threatened with death.
>
> *Jerusalem Post*, 11 November 1984

> Israeli Defender of Arab rights quits in 'Despair and
> Disgust'. Lawyer for Palestinians rarely won a case in
> 23 years.
>
> *Washington Post*, 13 May 1990

When she remembers the day that she dismantled her life, she remembers that a khamsin, the dry, hot, desert wind, was blowing through Jerusalem, through the streets, through the window of her office on Korresh Street as she locked the door where she had practised law for twenty-three years. Before she closed the door, there was the business of removing her life: taking down the pictures that her clients had drawn for her from prison, the poster of Nelson Mandela, her heavy, dark books of international law and the name-plate from her door that read Felicia Langer, Advocoie, the name-plate that was always being stolen or torn down. Then she hung her black lawyer's robes in a friend's cupboard in Tel Aviv, let her apartment and found a teaching job at Bremen University in Germany. After twenty-three years of defending the enemy Felicia Langer had had enough.

As she boarded a flight from Israel to Germany, she told friends that she would be back in three years' time. She said that she would not rest until there were two sovereign states, Israeli and Palestinian. Then she gave a press conference and said that she was no longer practising law because she was working in a lawless environment, a country without justice, and that she did not want the system to use her – a human rights lawyer – as a fig leaf.

She spoke slowly and clearly, and without a trace of subtlety. 'They always said, "You see, we are a democratic country. We have a Felicia Langer defending the enemy. You do not find such a thing in Syria or Jordan." I have decided that I will no longer be used like that. I will no longer be seen as legitimizing the system.

'I want my quitting to be a sort of demonstration and expression of my despair and disgust with the system, and maybe a proof that something must be done to grant protection to the Palestinians in the occupied territories,' she told the *Washington Post*, 'because for the Palestinians, unfortunately, we can't obtain justice.'

Langer was exhausted. Twenty-three years in the Israeli military courts, twenty-three years representing clients in cases that she knew she would lose, twenty-three years of documenting human rights abuses and hearing endless stories of loss and death and demolition and deportation showed on her face and in her eyes. The strain of commuting from her home in Tel Aviv to the airless courtrooms in the West Bank and in Gaza had left her emotionally drained. The offer to teach international law and human rights at Bremen University meant that she could spend more time with her husband and her only son, Michael, who had left Israel in 1982 to take up a job as a theatre director in Tübingen. No one was really surprised when she said she was leaving Israel. She was retreating. She had witnessed more than one should, and could, in a single lifetime.

'Do you know why Felicia Langer looks as tired as she does?' asked Ribhi al-Aruri, a former client. Al-Aruri is a Palestinian journalist who was jailed with three other Jewish editors during the *Derech Hanitzotz* case and later adopted by Amnesty

International as a prisoner of conscience. It was one of the biggest cases of 1988, concerning freedom of expression and state security, and obsessed Langer to the point, one of her friends said, of near frenzy. 'Because she has spent twenty-three years in the military courts,' al-Aruri said. 'That's a lifetime. Most people don't last three years.'

I had heard so much about Felicia Langer before I met her, most of it negative. The first reaction came from a friend, a Jewish woman I had known since I was fourteen whose mother is Israeli. At the mention of Felicia Langer my friend's face hardened. She delivered a lecture in a shrill and hostile voice: people like Langer, she said, were damaging to the state of Israel and, as a journalist writing about Langer, I too was damaging. I was anti-Semitic. Langer was anti-Semitic. She slammed down the telephone. We did not speak for six months.

My friend's reaction disturbed but also intrigued me. There were several different versions of the Felicia Langer story. One came from an Israeli television producer who considers himself 'a liberal Israeli' yet a Zionist at the same time. He talked about her with heavy sarcasm: 'Felicia the Great, our most famous communist,' he sneered. 'Do you know how much money she makes? A fortune.' At an Israeli sabbath dinner on a *moshav*, a collective community, I mentioned her name to a young couple and their two friends. One of the men was fresh out of reserve military duty in Nablus. His worst moments as a soldier in Nablus, he said, were defending himself against the children – the Palestinian children who stood on the walls of the Old City and dropped stones on to the heads of the soldiers. He said they were 'like ghosts, everywhere'. There were moments when he walked through the kasbah that he felt himself trembling with fear and nervous energy.

Rachel, one of the women there, was pregnant. She lowered

her eyes and said with soft alarm, 'What kind of Jew turns on her own people? What kind of Jew would help the enemy?'

I said, 'Why are the Palestinians the enemy?'

'This is our home and they want to take it from us,' said her husband, bristling slightly. 'It's very simple. When you are threatened, you have an enemy.'

'And where is their home?'

Rachel was a gentle, attractive woman who grew up on an apple farm in the Golan. Her Zionist grandparents had emigrated from Eastern Europe in the 1920s. Her childhood had been happy, rural and isolated; she remembered playing on the farm with her sisters, and later living on a kibbutz in the north. Then she recalled her days in the army with a kind of misty-eyed nostalgia: 'It was like a bunch of girls together, my growing-up time, the first time I was really on my own.' Her only contact with Palestinians had been with the workers on her family's farm and, after college, the merchants in Jerusalem. She was not racist. She was not ignorant. On the contrary, both she and her husband were well read, thoughtful and articulate. They had travelled widely and owned a small business in West Jerusalem.

Another voice from the table: 'They can go back to Saudi Arabia or Jordan. They are Arabs, and those countries are for them. This is a country for Jews.'

I asked if there could be two states in the area of Palestine or, as the Jews say, Eretz Israel, one for Jews, one for Palestinians.

'Not possible,' Rachel said, indicating the conversation was over. 'We will never, ever give up our land. My grandmother fought in the War of Independence in 1948. Before the intifada I was never afraid to walk down the street, even in Jerusalem. Now everything is changing. I'm not only afraid for us, but for our children. What kind of life do you think it is for us, to live in fear of terrorism, or of walking down the street and getting stabbed by an Arab?'

The subject was swiftly changed. I briefly thought of Meir Kahane, the late rabidly nationalistic rabbi and former head of the Kach Party, who once said, 'I don't hate Arabs. I love Jews. I wish the Arabs well – but elsewhere.' These people did not subscribe to Kahane's thinking, but their passion, and their unwillingness to compromise, startled me.

A young Israeli lawyer whom I met through friends knew Langer from the court system and said that he had often watched her in court. He remarked, 'Like most Israelis, I don't like her or what she stands for. She is a communist, remember. But I do admire her determination.' The one thing that struck him was Langer's professionalism. 'I was sure, the first time I saw her, that she would use all kinds of manipulation techniques in court. She didn't. I thought she'd cry and try to prevail with feminine wiles. She did not. She was highly professional, but at the same time full of passion.' He paused slightly. 'That's Felicia Langer's strongest and weakest point. Her passion.' When I told Langer what he had said about her passion, she smiled slightly. 'I am always falling in love with my clients, male, female, children. It's my biggest problem.'

A British radio journalist who had been based in Jerusalem for three years often saw Felicia Langer at press conferences. His theory was that Langer worked for the Shin Bet, the Israeli domestic secret police. I said that was absurd. 'But if it were, she would have unlimited access to exactly the sort of thing they want, and they pay a lot of money. I can think of no other reason why she should risk her neck for so long.' A Palestinian cab driver thought she worked directly for Yasser Arafat and probably had a hot line in her office to Tunis. 'Yes, she is very good friends with Arafat. I am sure that I saw a photograph of them together.' A Jewish friend in London said he thought Langer was brave and her work

A Palestinian man, suspected of PLO activities, stands in the ruins of his house after it was demolished by the Israeli army.

Unfinished houses for Israeli settlers.

Right: A Palestinian boy, wounded by a plastic bullet during clashes with Israeli forces, receives treatment in hospital in Nablus, West Bank.

Below: Palestinian women gather outside the same hospital as the wounded are brought in from the clashes.

A mother and her children in a West Bank refugee camp.

Left: Guela Della Rosa, an Israeli woman, grieves for her son (photograph in foreground). He was killed when his bus was fire-bombed by Palestinian youths.

Right: A Palestinian woman, with her husband and son, holds a photograph of her eldest son, who was killed by the Israeli army.

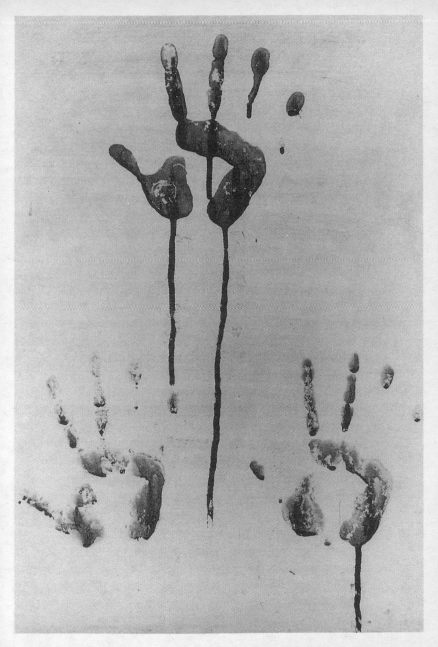

Handprints in blood on a wall in Nablus commemorate the deaths of Palestinian activists killed by special Israeli forces.

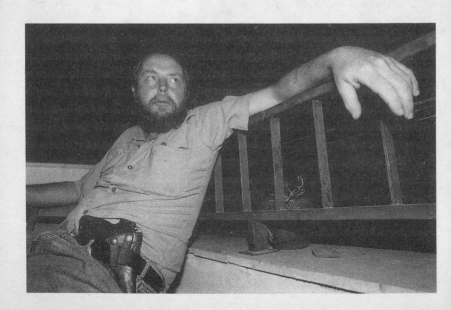

Right: Felicia Langer, the
Israeli defence lawyer, talks
with Roni Ben Efrat, the
left-wing Israeli journalist,
in Langer's Jerusalem office.

Below: Ed, a Jewish settler
from Chicago.

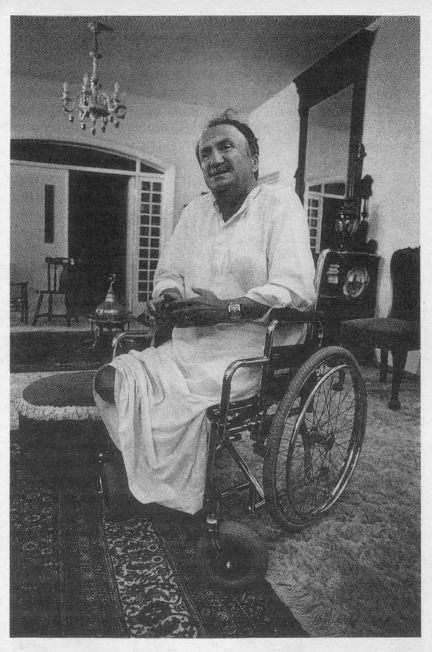

Bassam Shak'ah, the Palestinian ex-mayor of Nablus, who lost both his legs in an Israeli terrorist car bomb attack.

View of an Israeli town.

Late afternoon in Beach camp, Gaza Strip.

interesting, but that she was the sort of Jew who hates other Jews.

In November 1989 I wrote an article about Felicia Langer that appeared in Britain in the *Sunday Correspondent Magazine*. Almost immediately I received a letter from a reader regarding the 'pro-Palestinian activist':

Mrs Langer is much concerned about the present-day Palestinian suffering, but seems oblivious to the suffering inflicted on the Jews by the same Palestinians to whose defence she has devoted her life.

She sheds tears over Deir Yassin but has not one word of condemnation for the 1929 and 1936 massacres, the outrages committed by Arab 'irregulars' during the last months of the Mandate, the destruction of the Etzion bloc settlements or the ambush of the Mount Scopus convoy in 1948 when doctors and nurses were murdered by a frenzied Arab mob while the British army (responsible for law and order in the Mandate) chose to be late in coming to the rescue: she highlights what is happening today but ignores the historic context and all those events which led up to the present situation.

It would have been no more than fair for credit to be given ... to the Israeli judicial system which allows Mrs Langer to practise in the way she does without let or hindrance, and even to give interviews to foreign newspapers which only present half of the story. In the less democratic atmosphere of an Arab state she would no doubt find it more hazardous to pursue her self-appointed mission. There are, for example, hundreds of Jews held in the Islamic Republic of Iran who have been in prison for years without trial, with no one to defend them, simply because they are Jews: prisoners of conscience in the true sense of the word. To present their case to the Iranian revolutionary courts would surely be a very rewarding task for a person of Mrs Langer's zeal and ability, who is unable to stand human suffering. Not only would she be ideally suited to help her unfortunate co-religionists, to do so would also be an infinitely better chance for her to prove her mettle than the defence of the petty Arab terrorists under the watchful but indulgent eyes of the Israeli authorities.

The best answer about Felicia Langer did not come from a client or an enemy or a friend. It came from an old Palestinian farmer called Ali who lived close to the Mount of Olives, whom I met wandering near the Garden of Gethsemane. He asked me what I was doing in Jerusalem; I mentioned Felicia Langer. He smiled, his face crinkling into a mass of wrinkles. 'Ah, Felicia,' he said. 'She's always on television and she is always crying. I think she likes the Palestinians.'

A few months after she left Israel for her new home in Germany Felicia Langer received an award called the Right Livelihood Alternative Nobel Peace Prize from a foundation based in Stockholm. On 9 December 1990, her sixtieth birthday and the third anniversary of the intifada, Langer stood up before a crowd, shaking slightly with nervousness. She squinted and dabbed at her eyes, which are a curiously pale shade of blue and which have given her trouble since she arrived in Israel at the age of twenty. She claims it is the harsh sun that hurts them, the desert climate – or maybe, she said, it is because she is too thin skinned, or because she has seen too much.

'I am still too European, after all these years in this country,' she told me grandly when I first met her. Her skin is pale and slightly freckled and if she goes anywhere in a car in Israel, she always chooses the seat with the most shade and she almost always wears a hat and dark glasses. It is ironic that a woman who is so tough, and who is not frightened by anyone, is so physically delicate.

When I think of Felicia Langer, I have one perfect mental image of her that is as clear in my mind as a snapshot: she is walking slowly out of Ramla prison, near Tel Aviv, behind a massive security gate, wearing an enormous sun hat, wobbling on her high heels and weeping. I had driven Langer to Ramla to see a client, one of the *Derech Hanitzotz* journalists, in the hope that she would be released on early bail. Langer had failed and she collapsed in the back seat of my car crying, bunching her fists in frustration. 'They have no heart, they have no soul,' she said. 'They are made of stone.' On the drive back to Tel Aviv she hardly spoke at all.

In Stockholm Felicia Langer read slowly and carefully in English from a speech she had written at her desk in Tübingen when she knew that she had won the award:

the Palestinian tragedy, which is our tragedy too, is regarded as one of the most important topics on the international agenda, that it is unbearable to ignore the suffering of a whole people, denied basic human rights in the last decade of our century, a whole nation without protection. Blood is spilled daily all over the occupied territories and in Israel too, sometimes of innocent Israelis who are falling victims of Palestinians' revenge for the government's atrocities; a vicious circle of violence, turning us into a nation of killers and killed, a new Sparta of the Middle East, where the fathers are burying their sons.

Five weeks after the ceremony in Stockholm the Gulf War began. Langer was distraught, racked with grief, worry for her family and friends in Israel, and anger. Scud missiles were falling in Tel Aviv and the West Bank, Israelis were huddled together in their special sealed rooms every time a siren sounded and the Palestinians were openly backing Saddam Hussein. 'Why this bloody war?' Langer said twice, pacing, wringing her hands, twisting her heavy rings. 'Why now? What is it proving?'

In the midst of the Cable News Network reports and the anxious calls to Tel Aviv, two days after the United States declared war Langer went to Vienna to receive another honour, the Bruno Kreisky prize for human rights. It was the night after the first Iraqi Scud attack on Israel, and Langer had been up all night waiting by the telephone. I flew from London, and Heathrow Airport that night was deserted. It was peculiar not to queue up for my boarding pass or to have my luggage X-rayed. There were very few people on my flight; the stewardess said that most of them had cancelled that morning when they heard the news about the Scuds.

The ceremony took place mid-morning in the Rathaus on a freezing-cold but clear day, in an ornate and high-ceilinged room filled with dignified ladies in fur coats scurrying for seats on the red velvet chairs. I had walked to the Rathaus from my hotel, and the streets of Vienna were quiet. In the café where I had breakfast there was a solemn air as everyone scanned the newspapers for reports of the war. When I saw Felicia at the Rathaus, her eyes were red with fatigue and the cold, or maybe she had been crying, and she was moving through the room with a kind of pent-up energy. She was dressed in a suit and a silk blouse and gold jewellery, standing slightly to one side behind the podium, which emphasized how small she is. She looked vulnerable, slight, lost in the midst of the heavy fur coats and green loden hats. I had not seen her in more than a year and she kissed me firmly on both cheeks, leaving her bright-pink lipstick imprint behind, which she tried to rub away. Moshe, her husband, stood behind her with a video camera. She clung to his arm, swaying back and forth slightly.

'After all these years,' she said sardonically, gesturing to the crowd. 'Some recognition.'

During the presentation, which was in German, I sat near the back of the room, huddled into my coat, hands dug into my pockets for warmth. A woman in front of me wore an enormous fur hat, and I sat straight up to see over her head as Langer approached the podium to accept her award. Next to her was a strange man with the most unusual colour of hair: not quite grey, not quite brown, like that of a rodent. Several times he turned round to watch me take notes. During a break in the ceremony I made my way out into the hallway. I looked up: he was in front of me.

'Excuse me,' he said in a heavy German accent. 'What are you writing?' He stared at my notebook, which was bright red and embossed in black with the name of an American weekly news magazine. 'Are you American?'

I said that I was writing an article for a British newspaper, which I did not name, and that I was here to see Felicia Langer. At the mention of Langer the man smiled. He stepped closer: there was an unpleasant smell clinging to his clothes, like food that had gone off. Instinctively I stepped back. He dropped his voice; this time it was softer. 'Do you know Felicia Langer?'

I said that I did.

'She is a good woman, Felicia Langer, is that what you are thinking?'

I shrugged. He lit a cigarette and continued to smile. His teeth were rotten. He stared. 'I will give you some good information for your article. Do you know that Frau Langer is a Stalinist? When you return to London, why don't you ask the *Jewish Chronicle* to show you their files on Frau Langer? They will be delighted to tell you about her activities in Eastern Europe. Why don't you ask her why she let children starve in Eastern Europe and why she condoned the Czechoslovakian invasion in 1968? Why don't you ask her about Hungary, 1956?' He leaned closer to me. 'May I ask you, are you a Jew?'

I said that it was none of his business.

He laughed. 'Then maybe you hate the Jews? Because Langer is a woman who hates the Jews.'

I excused myself, walking back to my chair. He followed me, still ranting, cigarette smoke pouring out of his nostrils. He said (louder now) that he was qualified to speak on such subjects because he was a journalist and in fact worked for several British newspapers (he listed two, but later, when I checked, no one had heard of him). He claimed he had known of Felicia Langer and had followed her work for years. His interest in her, he said, was that he was also a Jew, and he wondered how any Jew could do the work that Frau Langer did.

'Excuse me,' I said for the second time and bolted towards the door.

He called after me in a loud voice, 'I ask you again. Why don't you ask Frau Langer why she hates the Jews?'

Inside, Frau Langer was standing in a crowd answering questions. Moshe was behind her with the video camera, watching with a patient expression as his wife argued in German with an older woman who wore a knitted hat. The woman was dabbing at her nose with a tissue. 'You, Frau Langer,' she shouted, pointing a finger, 'you should hang, Frau Langer! You should go to Saddam Hussein.'

Langer flushed heavily, but she leaned forward on the podium. 'As long as we have leaders like Shamir,' she said with force, 'there will be dictators like Saddam. As long as people like Shamir are in office, I will continue to attack the government. I am doing the best service for my country.' She moved closer to Moshe. 'This war is the worst thing that could happen to the Palestinians. There is no "policeman" in the occupied territories or in the world who renders help for the Palestinians,' she said. 'So they have seen Rambo, and it is Saddam and it is very sad. Believe me, this support of Saddam has made me sad, incredibly sad.'

The woman who said Langer should go to Saddam Hussein continued to shout. The German with the rotten teeth was behind her. 'Stalinist!' he hissed as we passed.

Langer sprang up. 'What did he say?'

'He called you a Stalinist,' I said.

The expression on her face did not change. If anything, she looked slightly amused.

Moshe Langer shrugged. 'It is always the same.'

For many years Moshe Langer ran an import–export business from Israel to the Eastern bloc countries. He is calmer than his wife. He survived five concentration camps and leads his life like someone who has seen the worst of the world and now wants to live life to the fullest. He shares his wife's convictions and oversees her work with a kind of quiet pride, a protectiveness that comes from living with someone for forty years and watching them continually put themselves into situations where they will be hurt. When I first met Langer, I asked her, 'But doesn't your husband mind you doing this work? When you are threatened or they try to run you over in a car, doesn't he mind?'

She looked slightly surprised, and answered awkwardly, 'No . . . he is my greatest support. It was my mother, who has since died . . . there were problems there . . . she was not always happy with my work.'

Now Moshe leaned over and pointed to the woman in the knitted hat and told me that he was certain she had been sent by the Israeli Embassy to harass Langer. 'We're sure of it,' he said. 'As long as Felicia speaks out, she will never have any peace. No, one thing is certain.' He shook his head. 'It has never been easy to be Felicia Langer.'

Felicia Weit was born in Tarnów, seventy-two kilometres east of Cracow, in Poland, in December 1930. Before the Holocaust the town was home to twenty-five thousand Jews and her parents were part of a middle-class Jewish intelligentsia – her father, Chaim, was a lawyer with two Ph.D.s, one in jurisprudence and

one in economics, and her mother was a genteel housewife. They
lived in a big house with a servant, and Langer remembers the
walks in the woods as a child with her father, and the way he
would quiz her on her studies. She recalls walking with him
through Tarnów; everyone would stop and greet him, and she
would have to say her two names, Felicia Amalia. 'He would be
so proud of me, if I got things right. It was a game, and I would
try so hard to seek his approval. He was my spiritual inspiration.'
She said that she has never cried so much as when she was
writing out the notes to her autobiography and had to dig back
into memories of her father.

'He was my first big love,' she says. 'All the loves that came
after stem from that love.'

Childhood, for Langer, is a warm and happy memory. They
observed Jewish holidays, but were, in her words, 'an assimilated
family'. She studied dutifully. 'My hunger, my striving for learning and always the thirst for knowledge comes from my father.
He cultivated that in me until he died.'

Like so many Polish Jews, her world changed irrecoverably
when Hitler marched into Poland in September 1939. She was
eight years old. When the war began, the family fled in terror to
the Soviet Union, first to the Ural Mountains, later Kazabhastan.
They had no food and all of them fell violently ill, but she
remembers the kindness of the Soviet peasants who shared their
little bits of food with them. 'I used to try to think, or maybe
someone told me, during those days, don't worry, don't worry,
you can see the gold even in the gutter.'

In 1944 Chaim Weid died of malnutrition. 'After that I was
dead, hungry, full of disease. I lost the love of life. For years I
longed for my father, I dreamt of him. One night, when I was
writing my book, he came to me in a dream. It was so beautiful,
I felt such a feeling of joy and elation. And then I woke up and it

was dark and it was night, and I had lost that happiness. And then I fell asleep again, and he appeared. Exactly as I saw him when I was a child. And then I woke again, and that joy was gone.'

In 1945, at the tail-end of the war, Felicia and her mother left the Soviet Union and returned to Poland. Searching for relations, they found no one; then they stumbled upon a Jewish cemetery and discovered that all of them had been wiped out. They rented a flat and struggled to piece together their lives. One night, at a youth club, Felicia met Moshe Langer, a locksmith, who had recently been released from Teresienstadt.

'I was very skinny from the war and I felt so ugly. Someone, when I was a child, implanted the idea that I was not attractive, so I had decided to use my intellect. That lasted until I was seventeen. Then I met my husband.'

Moshe Langer was eighteen years old and about seventy pounds when he was released. 'I survived because I never, ever doubted that I would live,' he says. 'It was an act of will.'

He first stayed with an elderly uncle in Cracow, 'but I had to leave because it was like a church. I had to be home by ten o'clock at night. So I escaped.' He moved to a home for young men without families, 'for orphans, because I was an orphan'. When he met Felicia Weid, he says that something instantly bonded between them. It was immediate and unbreakable, and they married on Christmas Day 1949.

Felicia was twenty when she and Moshe emigrated to Israel in 1950. Two years before, Britain's formal withdrawal from Palestine had resulted in civil war. Zionist resistance groups had united to capture Palestine and take major Arab towns. The British mandate formally ended on 14 May 1948 when the Zionists, led by Chaim Weizmann, proclaimed the foundation of the state of Israel. In 1949 the War of Independence ended with seventy-nine per cent of Palestine in Jewish control. Jerusalem was split between Arab East and Jewish West, and the Egyptians kept the Gaza Strip.

Under the Law of Return hundreds of thousands of Jews poured in from Eastern Europe, the Arab states, South and North America. For them, it was a heady, exciting time to be in the newly formed Jewish state. But for the Palestinians, many of whom were now refugees, it was a disastrous time, the era that they refer to as the nakbeh.

For Felicia Langer, going to Israel was not an easy decision. Her mother had remarried two years earlier and moved to Israel, and her new marriage was floundering. She pleaded with her only child to come. Langer was not a Zionist. She had wanted to stay in Poland to be a part of the post-war political restructuring, but she was torn by her commitment to her mother. 'There was excitement, romance and challenge in rebuilding a new society. I wanted to stay, but my mother needed me.' In the end she and Moshe packed their things and left Poland.

In Tel Aviv, where they settled, there were problems. There was the language barrier, the difficulties of learning Hebrew and forcing themselves to speak it to each other, and the fact that Felicia was not entirely comfortable in a capitalist country. In Poland Moshe had been a member of the Communist Party 'because I remembered the kindness of the Red Army to the survivors', and together they wandered into their first party meeting in Tel Aviv without an introduction. 'I wanted to be a part of something,' she says. 'I was very depressed at the time, and I had many ideals. The first time Moshe and I arrived at a meeting the other members were stunned, because no one just turns up, you have to be sent. They sat up, so surprised, and said, "Who are you? Who sent you to us?"'

By the time her son Michael was born in 1953, she and Moshe

had stopped speaking Polish to each other, and when Michael was old enough to go to elementary school, Felicia entered the faculty of law at the Hebrew University in Tel Aviv. She was twenty-nine, older than most of the students, and determined to succeed. 'In those days it was difficult to be a mother returning to school. It just wasn't done. But Michael and me, we went together. He went to elementary school and I went to university.'

She was not one of the best students in the class, but there was a drive and a passion to her work. Asher Bitan, who knew Langer from her student days, and is now one of the most renowned publishers in Israel, recalled that Langer at that time had the same kind of frantic energy, the determination always to do something. 'I remember seeing her in the student organizations. She was a communist then, always leading something, always with a kind of fiery passion. Even then, she had a cause.'

She was thirty-five when she began practising law, and had difficulty getting a job because of her membership of the Communist Party. She opened her own office in Tel Aviv and defended underdogs – juvenile delinquents, Arabs, Sephardic workers arrested for demonstrating. Two years after she opened her office, the Israelis won the Six Day War when Egypt entered the Sinai and closed the Straits of Tiran to Israeli shipping. Israel destroyed most of Egypt's air force and defeated the army in the Sinai; it controlled all Jerusalem and the remaining twenty-one cent of Palestine. The excitement and enthusiasm on the streets of Jerusalem following the victory was outstanding. In six days this tiny country had defeated its bigger, stronger, richer Arab neighbours. Israel seemed to be invincible.

If you ask Langer at exactly what point she became aware of the Palestinian situation, she says that it was the war. One day in 1967, shortly after the war, she stood looking at three destroyed Palestinian villages in the Latrun area, Yalu, Beit Nuba and Emmaus: 'Standing at the site, where I understood for the first time the meaning of the expression "not a stone remains", I took an oath to defend relentlessly the rights of the oppressed Palestinians. I already fully understood that the wrongdoers against the other people are the enemies of our people too.

'My life commenced in 1967. You cannot imagine the euphoria in Israel after the war. Suddenly it was Israel the conquerors! Israel the mighty. I did not feel in any way a part of it, I could not stand back and watch the injustice of the occupation of the territories. So I went there to fight the injustice of the system. I thought that I would be fighting for maybe one year, two years, and then we would have peace. I never thought I would be doing it for twenty-three years.'

She became the first Israeli lawyer to work in the occupied territories. Her first case was defending the son of a Palestinian imam (Muslim religious leader). She could not yet speak Arabic, and the Palestinian must have been amazed to find that his counsel was a tiny Israeli Jew and, even stranger, a woman. Her next few cases involved houses demolished by the army in Nablus; she saw it as ironic that the last case she tried before she left Israel for Germany was also the case of an Arab house demolished by the army.

For the next two decades she took part in some of the most important legal cases regarding Palestinians in Israel, and her name comes up in nearly every legal conversation about the occupied territories. The newspaper cuttings concerning Felicia Langer in the *Jerusalem Post* research library comprise a thick heavy stack, and it took me three days to sift through them. There were photographs of a younger, unsmiling Langer and a few of her clients. All the cases had an underlying thread: she would never defend a Palestinian who had killed civilians or someone who was actively dangerous.

In the 1970s, she took on one of Israel's most celebrated cases, which eventually became an enormous scandal and embarrassment for the Shin Bet. Palestinians who hijacked an Israeli bus died in custody and Langer represented the families. In 1974 she took the case of two Dutch students who were sentenced for serving as Fatah runners. In 1977, along with Leah Tsemel, another human rights lawyer, she was barred from appearing in court as defence counsel to two Germans and three Arabs accused of attacking an El Al jet-liner, because the military authorities regarded the two women as a security risk.

In 1977, in another widely reported case, she was the lawyer for a young Texan, Terry Fleener, who was accused of meeting Arab terrorists and sentenced to five years. In 1978 Langer was involved in leaking the story of Israeli torture of Palestinian prisoners to the *Sunday Times* Insight Team, which caused a major fracas in Israel. She participated in the highly volatile case of an Arab-American student, Sami Esmail, who, she claimed, was arrested without justification and tortured until he broke and signed a false confession. (She later 'adopted' Esmail and refers to him as 'my son'.) She met Yasser Arafat, infuriating officials. And she took on the long, involved case of Bassam Shak'ah, the former mayor of Nablus, whom the Israelis attempted to deport. He was the victim of an assassination attempt by the Jewish Underground terrorist group, which failed, but in which his legs were blown off. It is the Shak'ah case that she is closest to and that she regards as her greatest victory.

Benni Burger, the former director of B'tselem, the Israeli human rights lobby, and now a publisher, said that he does not agree with Langer's principles, but respects her integrity. 'If you look at any big legal case involving Palestinians since the occupation began, you will find Felicia Langer. She should get a Red Cross or something, because she did something for twenty-three years. She didn't make phoney revolutions, she went in to help people in the field.

'When I first saw her office, I was amazed, because it looked like the sort of place where someone would volunteer to work for four months. She stayed nearly twenty-five years and sacrificed her career, with no political motivation or egotism. She would get up in the morning and take on these small unromantic cases when it was an unpopular thing to do.

'You have to be one in a million to have that kind of determination. I envy her, because I don't have it.'

Langer accepted more cases than she could handle, and often ones that she knew she could not win. By the late seventies she began to see a terrible pattern emerging as the new generation of Palestinian youths and children grew up throwing stones and learning to hate the soldiers and see Israelis as oppressors; they knew no other life than that of the occupation. She recalled defending children in Nablus who had been throwing stones, and asking the judge to have a heart because they were children who could not bear the occupation any longer. 'He said to me, "What are you talking about? These children need to be taught a lesson." And so they were taught a lesson, and a whole generation was beaten and punished. And as a result, a whole people rose up.'

In 1979, partly to ease her own frustration, she began to keep a diary which eventually became her book *An Age of Stone*. In it she chastises her fellow Israelis for not acknowledging the inevitable:

They seemed genuinely surprised when the storm crashed out of the skies, when the Palestinians in the Occupied Territories rose up, when the mass of the people moved in pursuit of freedom after years of suffering and repression . . .

In spite of all the previous waves and the splinters of waves and the lightning and the thunder that announced its coming throughout the years, in spite of the decades of resistance to the occupation that did not cease for one single moment, in spite of everything, they could not foresee it.

In a sense Langer had never seen herself as extraordinary. She does not feel that it is odd for a Jew to do the work she does. The first time I met her I asked her, bluntly, why she did it. Was it ego? Was it a death wish? Was it because, as everyone inferred, she was not a proper Jew?

She looked at me carefully with her pale, watery eyes. 'I am a Jew, of course I am a Jew. And Israel is my country. But I am a human being first, and no human being can stand to see others suffer.' She fiddled with a piece of paper and arranged the piles of paper on her desk. 'Why do I do the work that I do?' she repeated wearily, as though she had been asked it a hundred times before. 'Because I am angry and sad, and obsessed. I suppose you would call it obsessed. I can't live in this country, my homeland, and see the suffering of another people caused by my own people. The executors are my compatriots.' She paused. 'To be silent is very, very wrong.'

The myth of Felicia Langer goes deeper. Her former clients said she was obsessed and emotional and driven; activists in the West Bank who named their children after her spoke of Langer as though she were superwoman trying to shield the masses.

'I think of her as my mother,' said Muhammed Z., an activist with a left-wing organization. He was sitting in his large house near Hebron drinking orange soda and smoking furiously. He had been ill; he was vague about exactly what was troubling him, but twice he got up and retreated to the bathroom. His mother, who brought coffee, biscuits and more orange soda, said that it had something to do with his stay in prison. On the shelf in Muhammed's bedroom were bottles and bottles of prescriptions.

'Before I met Felicia Langer,' he said, 'I read her book *With My Own Eyes*. There was a chapter on torture, on what it felt like to be inside an Israeli prison. Well, I have been inside and when I read that, I felt as though I had always known her. Then she became my lawyer. Any time I am released from prison I go straight to her office before I go home to Hebron to see my own mother. One time she came to see me in prison. I had not showered for forty days and I smelled so bad. But when Felicia saw me walking through the door, she grabbed me and kissed me and was crying. I had lipstick all over my face, and she was trying to wipe it off. Then the guard came and took me back to my cell and said to me, "Isn't she a Jew?" I said she was. He said, "So why is she representing you?"

'Sometimes I think she suffered more than us when we went to prison. She couldn't bear it because she is so idealistic. And she also suffered because of us. They were always threatening her, breaking into her office. Israeli society is not perfect, you know. They could do something like kill a lawyer and make it seem accidental. You can understand now why some of her clients call her Felicia the Great.'

I met Felicia the Great the next morning, in her office on Korresh Street. It was the beginning of April 1989, sixteen months into the intifada, and a few days into the Muslim feast of Ramadan, the month of fasting. In West Jerusalem the Jews were preparing for Pesach, the feast of Passover, and all the housewives were frantically cleaning out their houses and doing laundry, prompting the *Jerusalem Post* to write investigative articles about why women have nervous breakdowns around the time of Passover. In the streets, in the shops, even driving through the congested city there was a sense of feverish haste.

Earlier that week the tension between the Palestinians and the Jews in Jerusalem had been so intense that the then police inspector-general, David Kraus, went on record calling the clashes in East Jerusalem the worst since 1967. Outside Langer's office the streets of Jerusalem were steaming. The trouble began when Palestinian youths threw stones at Jews praying at the Western Wall, and ended some days after when a gunman dressed in an Israeli army uniform showered bullets on four teenage Palestinians sitting near the Jaffa Gate. Nineteen-year-old Khaled Shawish was killed and his three friends were badly injured: Mahmoud Zade, who was hit with five bullets, lay in his hospital bed and told reporters the killer 'was holding an Uzi and that's it. He didn't say anything to us and we didn't talk to him either. If I get my hands on him, I'll slaughter him.'

The Jaffa Gate murder was not the only incident that week. A few days later, in the early hours before dawn on 13 April, the Israelis sent border policemen to raid the village of Nahaleen, nestled in the Judaean hills south-west of Bethlehem. By the time the raid was over, five Palestinians were dead and twenty-five were wounded.

According to the villagers who accompanied the wounded to the hospital, the attack was premeditated – the paramilitary border police had been taunting the women of the village and firing shots at their homes, riding through the village calling out with a megaphone in Arabic, 'Come, bring out your sisters. I want to fuck them.' Some reporters who drove to the scene immediately afterwards said that it was one of the bloodiest single incidents to occur since the beginning of the intifada. The International Red Cross in Geneva was calling it a massacre, though when I wrote an article about it in a British paper, I at once received a letter from a reader: 'Where was the International Red Cross when Jews were being butchered in the Holocaust?'

The day after Nahaleen I went for a walk near Jaffa Gate in the late afternoon, about sunset. In Jerusalem there is no lingering sunset; the sun drops quickly, with no hesitation, and the sky is deepest blue, and then, very quickly, it is black. Outside the Jaffa Gate some Palestinian merchants were sitting cross-legged in front of their mats loaded with the most bizarre items: nail-files, toenail-clippers, combs, toothpaste, Old Spice aftershave. The money-changers were clustered together and a fat woman squatted in a corner selling Arabic sweets from a tray. The air smelled like rotted fruit.

There were small groups of Palestinian boys, in their late teens, leaning on the wall smoking cigarettes, and some Israeli soldiers watching them. I sat on an opposite wall of the Old City and watched the sky and the boys and the soldiers. The soldiers looked arrogant until you got close to them and saw that they were very young and bored or nervous as they held their guns at odd angles, playing with their watches or their leather bracelets. They could not possibly have wanted to be there.

The Palestinians seemed angry, and there was a stagnant feeling. I remained seated on the wall for a long time, until the sky was completely dark and there was only a sliver of moon, and the adan, the call to prayer from the minaret, had ceased and most of the Palestinians had left the wall to go home to break the Ramadan fast. Then the air was quiet and calmer and the soldiers more relaxed. I walked slowly back to East Jerusalem, past the Damascus Gate, past Nablus Road, past Saleh-al-Din Street with the shops barred and shuttered and littered with red and black graffiti, and down the hill towards Sheikh Jarrah, and then I went to bed and woke up at sunrise to the sound of the adan. The next day I met Felicia Langer for the first time.

'This is just one week in the history of the intifada,' Langer said, leading me into her office. It was a Sunday morning, early, and the first heat of the day was creeping into the room. I looked around, noted the dirty windows with dead philodendrons bordering them; the cramped space; the one telephone line and one frantic secretary answering it; the grey filing cabinets slightly open and bulging with papers; no computers; no coffee machine; the full waiting-room. Three Palestinians were sharing a copy of *Al-Quds*, the Arabic daily newspaper, while three more were knocking at the door. An earnest British law student, with little round glasses and a girlfriend in hippy sandals, had heard about Langer through Amnesty International and wanted her help to get them into Ansar 3, the detention centre in the middle of the Negev. 'Impossible, impossible,' Langer said tersely. 'No one gets into Ansar 3. I have a hard enough time getting in there to see clients.' A left-wing Israeli journalist who worked in an office downstairs dropped off a bundle of papers on her desk. There was a constant buzz of motion, of work, of time not being wasted.

It was definitely a myth, the story from the Israeli television producer that Langer made a lot of money. If she did, it was well hidden. The office was dusty, cramped and piled with books and papers. There were a few faded posters tacked up on the walls: Mandela with a raised fist, and another graphic one that said, 'The struggles of the past inspire the struggles of today.' I pointed to the poster and asked Langer if that meant the Holocaust. She cringed slightly.

'The period and the means of the Holocaust are incomparable,' she said slowly. 'But I was told by my husband that some of the methods used by the Israelis are similar to the methods used by the Nazis in the camps. The beating to death of people, the humiliation in prison, forcing them to bark like dogs, spitting in their mouths, beating sons before fathers, fathers before sons, doctors not being allowed to help the dying. It is compelling how it happened to us – to Jews – how we allowed it to take place in our country. But I'm not keen to draw comparisons, because they divert attention from the discussion. The facts speak for themselves.' She sat back heavily in her chair and rearranged a pile of papers. She was perspiring heavily and she wiped her brow.

She was not what I had expected. There were her unusual eyes – they were pale and translucent, like the eyes of a blind person. She was much more feminine than I had thought she would be. It startled me that Langer wore bright-pink lipstick and that she was dressed up in the Israeli equivalent of a power suit – blue, with shoulder pads – and a bright-coloured blouse. She was small and stocky, and her hands were little and freckled and covered with rings. Her dark-blonde hair was short but perfectly arranged and she patted it frequently. She wore a necklace and perfume. There was an air of vanity about her. I wrote down in my notebook: 'blue suit, necklace, make-up'. Langer watched me and, although she could not read the words, she said, 'People are always surprised when they meet me that I am so feminine. They expect something different.'

Langer fanned herself with her hand. Her fingernails matched her lipstick. The room was stifling hot; there was a small enclosed balcony overlooking the Old City walls, but there was no fan in the office. My hands were so sticky from the heat that they kept sliding down my pen. I looked up from my notebook and saw her. 'You have come to Israel at a terrible time,' she said in heavily accented English. I smiled, not knowing whether she meant the dense heat or the intifada. She did not return the smile. She said, 'These are very dark days.'

Felicia Langer had seen the intifada coming long before, but first realized that something devastating was going to happen when she began to represent the children of her former clients.

She calls them the second wave. 'I felt the storm a long time ago, because of my knowledge and experience of working with the Palestinians. They looked patient, but it was a special sort of steadfastness. They have a very inventive nature in the way that they oppose the occupation. Therefore, the storm had to happen. It's like the ninth wave in mythology, the most powerful wave, the one that wipes everything out.'

The telephone rang and Langer told me, brusquely, to wait outside while she took the call. As I shut the door, she began speaking rapidly in Arabic, shouting. I sat on a fake-leather chair, dangled my legs and leafed through a copy of *Al-Quds*, which the Palestinians had left behind when they went into her room. Through the closed door I could still hear her shouting. I asked Maha, Langer's secretary, if I could have a photocopy of a court report that Langer was working on and Maha replied, 'Yes, but you'll have to give me some shekels, because we don't have any money.' I gave her some coins and she turned from me to get the records.

'Let me tell you something about Fula,' Maha said, using Langer's nickname. 'She is not a woman that is liked.' She methodically ticked off various incidents on her fingers: 'There was the time she was in court and twisted her ankle and they would not treat her at Hadassah Hospital because she was Felicia Langer. The time that a car swerved deliberately off the road and tried to hit her. The time the secretary before me came into work and there was a message from Meir Kahane: "The day of your death is near, you whore of the P.L.O."'

Maha said for a while Langer had a bodyguard, but could not afford to keep him. 'Sometimes she works late here and instead of going back to Tel Aviv, she sleeps on a couch in the office. That is when I really worry about her.' She handed me the photocopy and warned me not to take too much of Langer's time. 'She is so busy and she is tired. She did not sleep at all last night because of the case. She is obsessed again.'

The door to Langer's office flew open and the three Palestinians shuffled out. One wore a black leather glove on his hand despite the heat, and I stared at it. Langer appeared and called me back in, motioning towards the chair.

She was working on a case that involved the three men. They were the family of 34-year-old Ibraheem Mtour, who was detained in prison and later found hanging in his cell in October 1988. The authorities claim he killed himself. Langer and his brothers say he was murdered.

She had battled endlessly with the Supreme Court for a repeat autopsy, and finally set a judicial precedent by receiving permission to have Mtour's body exhumed. An outside pathologist had flown in from Scotland to re-examine the case, the first time the Israeli High Court of Justice allowed the reopening of a Palestinian grave.

A few days later the exhumation took place. Langer lay on the couch in her office, too exhausted to travel back to Tel Aviv and Moshe, but emotionally unprepared to go to the West Bank and witness the opening of the grave. The family was not happy about it. They believed that Ibraheem came from Allah and he went to Allah. The mother was hysterical, refusing to give permission. Finally a brother signed the papers and the grave was opened at night, after the Israeli-imposed village curfew, quietly so that the villagers would not know. In her office Langer waited for hours by the phone. 'All night, I saw his face, the body, over and over in my mind . . . I remembered the first time I saw a photograph of Mtour after he died and I couldn't go through it again.'

By the end of the week the pathologist concluded that Mtour – who had been kept in solitary confinement, shackled, force-fed drugs and tear-gassed – 'may have been killed'.

The rather uncertain phrase 'may have been killed' pleased Langer: she said it was a small ray of hope. 'They allowed the exhumation only because they realized it was an unnatural death. That in itself is a positive sign.' It seemed like a very minor victory to me, but Maha said those tiny victories were the only thing that kept Langer going.

'She is more than a lawyer,' Maha said, handing me three bound legal documents on the case. 'She's a psychiatrist, a social worker, a mother. The people love her because she suffers with them.'

There are now others who do the work that Langer did, though not exactly in the same context – Tamar Peleg, who did not become a lawyer until she was in her sixties, works primarily in Gaza, and Leah Tsemel, married to the left-wing activist Mikado Warschawski, works out of an East Jerusalem office. But when Langer started defending Palestinians in the military courts in 1967, she was the only one. In the early days of the occupation Moshe would drive her to the airport in Tel Aviv and put her on a small plane to the Golan Heights. The planes were small and rickety, and Moshe would worry about her from the moment that she kissed him goodbye and walked, trembling, on to the ramp. Inside the plane she would cling to her seat. Moshe remembered this: 'Every time she got up in one, I was never really certain that she would land.' Langer would spend the day in the Golan with her clients, and then fly back to Tel Aviv and appear in the Military Court.

She does not like talk about the past. There is too much to be done with the present, she would say, and turn to a case that she was handling that day, or a speech she was going to give, or tell me, impatiently, to look up the case in the newspapers. When she does talk about the past, she does it slowly and painfully, but the clarity with which she recollects details is astounding.

Sometimes she thinks back to a particular case that has what she will call 'a happy ending', and then she will talk, her eyes misting, her hands fidgeting nervously in her handbag, pulling out her sunglasses, her lipstick, reapplying the bright pink to her lips using a tiny mirror she always keeps there. She is never still. 'It is a very sad and very long story,' she would say, or 'It is a very beautiful story.' Then she would talk, quickly, in English, occasionally stumbling to find the right word.

The case of Bassam Shak'ah, the former mayor of the West Bank city of Nablus, is one that she is willing to discuss. She likes to point out that their birthdays are only one day apart and that the happiest day of her life was when Bassam was released from detention after the Israelis tried to deport him. 'I have never felt such joy.'

'If you want to know about my life and my work, you must talk to Shak'ah,' Langer told me one day.

I saw Shak'ah for the first time at the beginning of the intifada when Nablus was the hub of most of the West Bank activism, and there were constant strikes, roadblocks and police checks. I drove to Nablus with Mustafa, a Palestinian photographer who wore a dirty brown two-piece suit and open-toed sandals, leaving early in the morning from Ramallah. I drove; he wanted to meet a Palestinian journalist who worked for a local wire service in the town square at half past nine. I arrived a few minutes late at the meeting point in Ramallah, and Mustafa was pacing nervously up and down.

That day was a strike day in the West Bank and the roads were empty. I ate an orange on the way up, and drank a bottle of mineral water, feeling faintly guilty because Mustafa was fasting for Ramadan and would not even take water. He looked out of the window. I asked him if he was hungry. He said it was no problem. 'It is for Allah.'

The other journalist, a small woman about the same age as I am, was called Amal. She was extremely edgy. When we pulled up alongside her in the deserted square in Nablus fifteen minutes late, she leaped into the car and asked Mustafa to change places with me and drive through the centre of town. I said that was ridiculous, nothing was going to happen; but I saw the look on her face, so I got out and let Mustafa drive. Amal nudged Mustafa on his arm, urging him to drive through the square as quickly as possible. 'I don't want to sit here for long.' Mustafa turned down a side street and we went into her office to pick up some papers. Her office consisted of a Formica desk with a typewriter, a stack of *Al-Quds*, an English dictionary and a pile of pamphlets. There was a telephone and a man she introduced to me as 'my husband', talking rapidly in Arabic. Amal picked up her papers and said we were going to Nablus Hospital. There had been a clash with the army at a demonstration and there were casualties. She had to get the names and ages of the 'martyrs' and the wounded to an East Jerusalem newspaper by lunchtime, and she was tense. She picked at a hangnail and refused my offer of a cigarette.

We drove slowly through the quiet streets, winding our way to a small white building on the hill, the hospital. Outside was a group of Palestinian women in long dresses and headscarves, wailing. Amal jumped out and Mustafa and I followed, pushing our way through the crowd, into the hospital lobby, which was packed with more women, screaming, one doctor, two male nurses and the flat pale body of a seventeen-year-old who came in on a stretcher with a bullet wound two inches above his heart.

Blood eased from the wound, and I was surprised at how slowly it pumped out of him. The boy's eyes were open; he was in shock, but he made no sound at all. The male nurse was smoking, and his white coat was filthy. When a car arrived with more bodies, the woman next to me let out a high-pitched shriek and another woman grabbed my arm and told me that after a clash the Israeli soldiers deliberately blocked the road with trees so that the wounded could not be brought directly to the hospital.

Three more cases came in, broken bones sticking out through flesh. The boy on the stretcher was the worst casualty. He was beginning to shake violently, and as the stretcher passed me, I looked down into his face. He returned the stare, his eyes glazed with pain, and Mustafa put the camera directly in his face and then rewound his roll and gave it to a nurse to put in her sock in case the army arrived.

They put the boy with the bullet wound in an operating room with the only doctor, and the door was shut. Mustafa followed. A child was brought in, a three-year-old boy who had been shot in the hip with a plastic bullet during a demonstration. The hole was minute and perfectly round and there was not much blood, but the boy was crying and waving his small fist, and the women raised their screams to a deafening level. Someone grabbed the boy and brought him into another room. The mother tried to follow, but was stopped at the door. The male nurse with the dirty white coat leaned against the wall with me and lit a cigarette. 'What kind of animal would do this to a child?' he said.

I knew how some Israelis might respond: what was a three-year-old doing at a demonstration where there was shooting and stone throwing? I said nothing.

Amal was using a telephone in the hallway. She said she wanted to show me something and led me up the back staircase to the wards, past the young boys sitting on blankets selling fruit and soap and aftershave, and into the patients' rooms, which were incredibly dirty, with peeling paint and filthy floors. In the halls were used bedpans and trays of rancid-looking dishes of yoghurt and hummus and copies of Arabic newspapers. There were eight or ten beds to a room, all of them filled with young shabbab, who had been shot, beaten up, tortured, run over. Collar-bones had been stamped upon, legs shot near the knees, the thighs, the ankles, fingers broken from being pulled out of their sockets, faces smashed in from clubs. There were black eyes, swollen noses. We walked quickly through the rooms, with Amal taking the names of all the boys and where the clashes had been. Every few minutes she would turn round and make sure that I was writing. She wanted me to know, she told me aggressively, what they had to live with, the sort of work she had to do everyday. 'It is not something you get used to,' she repeated at every bedside.

We left the hospital and drove to Bassam Shak'ah's house in silence. Amal's mood had begun to affect Mustafa, who decided it was best to go back to Jerusalem before we were stopped by the army. He said that his photos of the hospital were too good to lose and that it would be pointless to risk having the army confiscate them. Amal played with her thumbnail. Mustafa said, 'If you have good pictures, you have to know when to stop.' I said I wanted to see Shak'ah, and since I was driving, we continued up to the house on top of the hill, past the shuttered, gutted buildings splashed with graffiti, the empty market, the stretches of wasted land.

'Shak'ah is watched by the army constantly,' said Amal. She tapped her foot against the floor. 'They were at his house yesterday.' She pointed to the hills above, where there was a clear outline of soldiers watching through binoculars on tripods.

I said that she was not in danger and that nothing could happen to her.

She was silent. 'Nothing will happen to you. You have a press card, a passport. They can shoot me.'

'They won't shoot you,' I said. She said mothing.

We pulled into Shak'ah's driveway in front of his house, a marbled, massive Arabic-style home. His family had owned a soap factory in Nablus for years, and before 1948 they owned orange farms. They are wealthy Palestinians who have always been able to travel, send their children to university abroad, get medical treatment in Jordan, drink good Scotch whisky. Their lives are worlds apart from the refugees in the camps around the city of Nablus: Balata, Askar, Fara'a, Camp No. 1.

When the car stopped, a Palestinian child of about seven years old interrupted his soccer game and ran over and handed me a leaflet. Amal grabbed it from my hand, read it, turned white and began to shriek in Arabic at the child. 'It's forbidden, forbidden! Do you understand? It's an underground document. DO NOT HAND THESE OUT ON THE STREETS!'

The child, startled, ran away. Amal shredded the paper and tossed it in the gutter after casting a glance over her shoulder to see who was looking. 'They are crazy! In broad daylight, with the army watching our every move!'

Mustafa, tired from fasting for Ramadan and all the emotion at the hospital, tried to placate her. 'They're only kids. It's nothing, really.'

'The intifada is nothing?' she shouted. 'What are you saying?'

Mustafa shrugged.

I was silent and walked ahead of the two of them to the house where Shak'ah sat waiting for us in his wheelchair, his hand extended for me to take. The stumps of his amputated legs were fully visible under his long white robe, and he was fingering worry beads. When he shifted his weight, he moved his galabiya over the stumps and you could see the stitches.

Shak'ah was born in December 1930 into a family of five brothers and six sisters. His earliest memory was of the first

Palestinian uprising against the British in 1936. As a student at the An-Najah School in Nablus he became active in Palestinian nationalism, and established himself as one of the young leaders of the resistance against the Jordanian occupation of the West Bank. As a result, from 1957 he was constantly monitored by the Jordanian authorities. He drifted from country to country to avoid them, but by the time he turned twenty, he had made a conscious, political decision, understanding the consequences. He felt that he had a responsibility: to liberate Palestine.

Shak'ah went underground for two and a half years in Syria; he briefly joined the Baath Party but resigned in 1959, after the split between Egypt and Syria. In 1961 he married Anaya en-Fassa, also from a large established Nablus family, and one year later he was imprisoned in Syria. After being deported to Lebanon with his family, he was moved to Egypt as a 'political refugee'.

'Then the Jordanian government stopped following political leaders and in 1964 we returned home. We had a family – the oldest girl born in Damascus, the next in Cairo, and the last two in Nablus.' He was again imprisoned in Jordan in 1966, and after the Israeli occupation in 1967 the authorities made repeated attempts to deport him, all of which failed.

Shak'ah became mayor of Nablus in 1976. 'In 1979 I was called to the office of the minister of defence and he threatened me. He said, "You shall face physical punishment." I told him I had a political responsibility and a civilian duty. He warned me again.'

A few days later Shak'ah got a call from the military governor of the civil administration. According to Shak'ah, the governor also threatened him, saying, 'You shall face the worst thing you can dream about.' The worst thing to a Palestinian is deportation, because it means they are cut off from family, from friends, and can never again return to their home. Shak'ah knew that the authorities were planning his deportation and sat by the telephone with Felicia Langer, waiting for the news. 'We knew it would happen, at any time. Felicia would phone me every hour with reports: in the Knesset, they said this, in the Knesset, they said that. Everybody was ready.'

Shortly after his meeting with the defence minister the first blow fell: Shak'ah was arrested and detained for twenty-six days in Ramla prison, outside Tel Aviv. He refused to cooperate with the authorities: for two weeks he went on a hunger strike in protest at his solitary confinement; at the end he was force-fed. Langer put forth an application for an order nisi to rescind the deportation order, and obtained an interim order to stop the deportation process temporarily. Afterwards she received a recommendation from the Military Advisory Board to stop the expulsion order against Shak'ah. The order was cancelled by the military governor. Until then the board had never rescinded a military order of deportation.

It was an extraordinary outcome, and Shak'ah went back to Nablus with a hero's welcome. In his sitting-room in Nablus today is a black and white blown-up Associated Press photograph of his return, with a younger smiling Shak'ah being hoisted into the air by a crowd of jubilant supporters. That happiness was short-lived. Soon after he began to be pressured by the authorities to resign as mayor. He blatantly refused. 'I told them that I would rather be dead.'

On 2 June 1980 three bombs were planted by the Jewish Underground, an ultra-right-wing terrorist group headed by a group of settlers, among them Moshe Zar. They were carefully designated: one was left in Nablus for Shak'ah, one for the mayor of the West Bank town of al-Bireh and one for the mayor of Ramallah. The mayor of Ramallah lost one foot and mobility in his leg; the mayor of al-Bireh was lucky – he decided not to drive his own car to work that day. Shak'ah was the worst casualty.

He was on his way to his office in the early morning. Leaving his family in the kitchen, he got into his car, put the key in the ignition and felt the force as the bomb exploded. He remembers that his body was thrown from the car, but he did not immediately lose consciousness. It was like looking at everything in slow motion: 'My body felt empty. I saw the car and saw it smoking, and wondered if I could drive myself to the hospital. I stared down at my legs – there was nothing there – and I saw the blood. My hands did not work. I saw the flesh and blood on the ground.' Another bomb had been planted inside the garage in case the first one did not work; when it was later defused by an Israeli soldier ('a Druse, they sent an Arab Israeli to do it'), the second bomb exploded and blinded him.

Inside the house Shak'ah's wife was having breakfast with the children. She heard the noise, but thought it was an aeroplane passing overhead. A neighbour going by on his way to work found Shak'ah lying on the ground and, falling beside him, began to weep. Shak'ah was still conscious enough to say, 'Don't cry, get an ambulance, and tell my sons to warn the other mayors about the bombs.' That is the last thing he remembers before he lost consciousness.

The telephone wires to his home had been cut, so his son ran to a neighbour who brought a car and drove Shak'ah's limp and bleeding body to the hospital. On the way he woke up once, looked at his wife and said, 'Allahu Akbah', God is great. Then he passed out again.

Three hours after the surgery he insisted on letting journalists into his room. The doctors refused, but Shak'ah said if the press did not report the incident, he would rip the intravenous wires from his arm. His mutilated legs were developing gangrene; he was in agony. Three days later what remained was amputated. His family took him to Amman for further treatment; one month later he returned to work in Nablus.

He was determined to continue his work, that the amputation would not affect him, that he would not cave in to the Israeli authorities. He was in constant pain. His wife was frantically worried. 'I went to England for five months to have artificial legs fitted. When I returned, the real active aggression began. I was watched for twenty-four hours a day, I was under house arrest. This went on for five years. Anyone who shook my hand, said hello, offered to drive me through Nablus was harassed. The soldiers came to my wife when she was in the garden and said, "You whore, we shall fuck you." I went to the military government to protest, and they sent the same soldier who said it to her to my house to guard me. The ultimate humiliation.'

Shak'ah was continually pursued by the army. A group of soldiers appeared on his doorstep, jeering, 'If we didn't get you last time, we'll get you next time.' When I later asked an Israeli soldier, who had served in Nablus around the same time, who was responsible for the accident, he gave the thumbs-up sign and grinned. 'Our side,' he said proudly. Once, during a family lunch, one Israeli soldier jumped into the garden and urinated on the flower-beds while his comrades cheered him on. Another time, while the family sat in the garden, the soldiers came in, stripped off all their clothes and sunbathed naked. The Israeli authorities consistently deny the harassment.

'When one of my daughters was six years old,' Shak'ah said, 'a soldier stopped her on the way to school and showed her the photograph of a man with his eyes cut out. She came home crying, and I said, "Why do you cry? Go out and insult them." After that she went out and threw a stone. I told her there are many stones, many ways, to defend yourself.'

In 1982, shortly before Israel invaded Lebanon, Shak'ah was dismissed as mayor of Nablus when the civil administration decided that they wanted to direct daily life through military law. He is the last elected mayor of Nablus; after he was dismissed, there were no more Palestinian elections. 'And that is the Palestinian battle,' he said, wheeling himself into the house. 'They want to destroy not just the body but the mind. Today, for instance, my wife is in Jerusalem shopping, but I never know when or how or even if she will return. This is the daily life, the kind of worry that anything might happen again. After the assassination attempt, there was no formal investigation.

'I am still alive, and I can still continue to struggle. When I lost my legs, I became closer to the struggle, to the land. What happened to me,' he said, smiling broadly, 'is that I wanted to defend my city, to make life better, to help my people. That is my crime.'

Shak'ah first met Langer in 1976 when she was visiting Nablus prison. 'She was crying as she explained the treatment of the prisoners. One of her clients had a cigarette stamped out on his face. When my deportation trial arose, she faced great hostility. I was the only Palestinian at that time whose deportation was stopped.'

From his wheelchair, Shak'ah now watches the intifada with a careful eye. In 1989 he was given a human rights award, along with Nelson Mandela, by the Alphonso Committee in Madrid. At the time the intifada was sixteen months old and the towns of the West Bank were united in active resistance. Despite Shamir's heavy-handed restraints, the intifada was flourishing with popular committees.

'The peace initiative does not rule out suppression of the intifada,' Shamir told reporters, referring to his proposals for 'free and democratic' elections in the occupied territories. 'We extend one hand for peace and have the other hand free to strike at the rioters.'

'But if Shamir thinks that he can suppress the uprising, he is very, very wrong,' Bassam Shak'ah said to me, sitting up very high in his wheelchair. 'Because, as Palestinians, we are born into darkness and it gets darker and darker. For us, the intifada is the light at the end of the tunnel.'

I visited Shak'ah again in late 1991, by which time the direction of the intifada had changed drastically. Most of the leaders had been jailed, the universities had been closed, only to be briefly reopened and then closed again, the Gulf War had destroyed morale, the momentum seemed shattered. When asked by *Challenge*, the magazine of the Israeli Left, in November 1991 whether or not the intifada should go on, the Palestinian intellectual Sari Nusseibeh replied, 'I like honesty. For the last two years we haven't had an intifada, but the resistance of a few.'

Shak'ah disagreed. He did not feel, as many Palestinians did, that the intifada was breathing its last breath, but that it was in a different stage. 'The intifada is necessary to our future like food is to anybody. The struggle is our national food.'

At the time of the Gulf War I asked Felicia Langer the same question. Was the intifada over? She was distracted, thinking of something else, but she turned and fixed me with a stare. 'At first they said it would be over in a week,' Langer said. 'But this week has lasted for months and now there is still no sign that it will end. But there is one thing that you can be sure of. The intifada is the most important event in the last decades in the history of the Middle East. We, the Israeli people, will one day be grateful that the Palestinians shook us up from our delusions, our false dreams.'

One year after she left Israel Langer went back to launch her autobiography, *Fury and Hope*, in Israel. She was worried about the reception. Would she be ignored because she is Felicia Langer? Would the book sell? She had written five other books, but this was the most sensitive. 'This is my story,' she said defensively. Still, her agent had trouble booking her on television shows – she is too controversial. When journalists came to interview her, they wanted to talk about why she had recently left the Communist Party, after nearly forty years of membership. It was a touchy issue. 'I don't want to talk about it,' she said bluntly. She became disillusioned with the party, she said as we were driving to Nazareth to visit her old friend the mayor. 'Too much has happened.' Her name still conjures up varied reactions. In a Tel Aviv publishing house I met an Israeli journalist who bristled at Langer's name and said that she was 'obscure and extreme', that most Israelis would view her as radical. She suggested I find other, 'centred' lawyers to write about. She did not, she said, respect Langer. She eyed me with suspicion. 'She does not give a good picture of Israel.'

I picked up a copy of Langer's new book and walked home slowly through Tel Aviv. The West Bank seemed light-years, rather than a few miles, away. The peace talks were gearing up to take place in Madrid and, although the newspapers and television reported nothing else, the people did not want to discuss them. It was September, the month of Jewish holidays. One woman told me that she was 'tired of talking about politics. I've spent the last three years marching against something, demonstrating against something else, hoping for the peace talks. Now they get here and I'm tired.' She sighed. 'Frankly, I have had enough.'

Early one morning Felicia Langer rang me in my hotel in Tel Aviv. I was lying in bed reading a book I had found the night before, an Israeli travel guide from 1950 called *In the Land of Milk and Honey*. As I talked to her, I watched a tiny white mouse run in between two chests and disappear into a hole. I threw my book at it; Langer asked what the noise was.

She spoke loudly, switching from English to German, which she had recently learned. 'To be here again, in my home, you have no idea how happy I am!' She said that she had arranged to see all her old friends, Bassam Shak'ah, the mayor of Nazareth, her friends in Gaza and in the Golan Heights. She had felt emotional from the moment she got off the plane, frequently on the verge of tears. 'The heat is bothering me,' she said and asked if I had been in the sun. I replied that I had and she sucked in her breath and lectured me on the Middle Eastern sun. 'You will ruin your skin for ever.' She told me I should use sunblock at all times, 'at least number twenty-one', and that she would meet me at ten o'clock sharp the next morning in front of her old flat in Jerusalem to go and see Shak'ah. She said goodbye, slightly confused, in German, and slammed down the phone.

The next day Felicia and I sat in the back seat, out of the sun, while Moshe sat in the front with Shak'ah's driver, who had been sent from Nablus to collect us. We took the old road, through Tel Aviv and the West Bank, winding through hills and valleys as the mist lifted. Langer stared out of the window, lost in thought. Next to her was a large box of sweets she was bringing for Shak'ah.

Moshe was talking quietly to the driver, an old Palestinian and friend of Felicia, who was overjoyed to see her. 'And do you remember, Fula, the time we drove home through a strike, and we had to dodge all the Molotovs and the stones? And the window got shattered and they threw so many stones?'

Felicia remembered, and told her version of the story, of driving home late at night, avoiding the burning tyres and Molotovs and the stones, and how tired she was and how she kept thinking about having to get up the next day for a big case in the military courts. The story seemed to make her happy. She was smiling, looking out of the window and repeating, 'I am home!' Then she started laughing excitedly. 'But how is Shak'ah, tell me, how is my good friend, Shak'ah?' When we arrived in Nablus, driving past Balata refugee camp, she grew restless and began to fidget, pulling cosmetics out of her bag one by one and making up her face, though it was already perfect. She handed me a tube of Lancôme sunblock with advice: 'I take it everywhere.'

When we pulled up into Shak'ah's driveway, Langer leaped out before the car had stopped. She raced out to Shak'ah and kissed him firmly on both cheeks. She was crying, but she was happy. The two looked at each other carefully. Moshe ran up the hill and began filming, his camera leaning on a tripod. I sat on the side and watched, thinking about the strange friendship between the two: a Palestinian activist and a Jewish lawyer. Langer called him her 'best friend'.

Shak'ah moved his wheelchair to the veranda where his family – a brother, his wife, a cousin and his wife – were sitting. The cousin was smoking a hookah and it made a rumbling sound as we crossed on the grass. Then there were more kisses as Langer sat down, and Moshe kept filming. We went inside, into Shak'ah's ornate living-room; a large bottle of Johnny Walker Red was poured and Langer held out her glass: 'Just a little.' She drank it quickly and had another. Shak'ah's wife produced an enormous lunch, and afterwards plates and plates of water melon and more drinks were served. Langer was laughing and talking in Arabic and English. It was dusk when we left Nablus, hurrying because the driver had to take us to Tel Aviv and return to his city before curfew.

Langer took the back seat. 'I must sleep,' she said. I sat in the middle of the Mercedes sedan and saw the hills darken, the

Palestinian workers coming home to the West Bank from their jobs in Tel Aviv, the big cars full of Jewish settlers driving to Ariel, two Australian travellers with a flag on their backpack waiting at a bus-stop. What were they doing in the middle of the West Bank? We drove past the refugee camps, the sloping hills, the villages, and then into another world, Tel Aviv. Here there were Day-Glo surfers on skateboards, children sucking on ice-cream cones; tourists from New York and South Africa looking in the shop windows, buying gold jewellery and antique menorahs and Persian rugs; soldiers on holiday with their guns slung across their backs, and their arms around their girlfriends; vendors selling felafel.

Langer slept soundly in the back. 'She is happy,' said Moshe. He was singing softly. Near the beach in Tel Aviv the driver stopped to let me off at Ha-Yarkon and I gathered my things quietly so as not to wake her. But she sat up as I opened the door and wiped her eyes. She looked around, realized we were in Tel Aviv and squinted slightly. She told me, in a determined voice, to be sure to use sunblock. She said she would look forward to the day when she would come home, but until then, she would continue working from Germany, teaching human rights and international law at the university, lecturing, building up support for the Palestinians and the Israeli peace forces. She sank back into sleep and I watched the car drive away.

Some time later I heard from her by fax in London. In the late spring of 1992 the occupied territories surged with a new kind of lawless violence and there was a rash of killings in Gaza and the West Bank. In May a settler was stabbed to death in Gaza, and I stared at the funeral on television, the sorrow on the faces of the children and the anger and hostility of the crowd. Collaborator killings soared. Palestinian women in Nablus were being tortured and hacked to death by their own people on suspicion of collaborating with Israelis. The Middle East peace talks were going nowhere. June marked the twenty-fifth anniversary of Israel's victory in the Six Day War and the occupation. So much had happened in the beginning of the intifada, but nothing, it seemed, had changed. There were still the Palestinians on one side and the Israelis on the other.

There was a wistful quality to Felicia's letter. 'My dear Janine, You see, the tragedy is still going on,' she wrote in her slanted old-fashioned handwriting. 'The news from Israel and occupied territories is terrible. How long will the people suffer? I am sometimes so terribly tired from my endless trips for lectures, but the news gives me new energy and strength to try to help the people as much as possible, to disseminate the truth and alarm. I still believe in humanity. Yours, Felicia.'

4. Dreams

Among us, even dreams are crushed under the weight of reality.

David Grossman, *The Yellow Wind*

One of them printed his message on the sides of more than one hundred Israeli tanks – an appeal to his fellow reservists to refuse to serve in the occupied territories. Some of the women wear black dresses and stand vigil beneath signs demanding Israel's withdrawal from the West Bank and the Gaza Strip. More than twenty of the men have gone to jail as conscientious objectors . . . They are a new and sometimes radical breed of Israeli dissidents whose forty-odd groups have proliferated in response to the Palestinian uprising. So far, they are too few and too disunited to have much visible impact on Israeli politics. Nonetheless, many dovish Israelis who disapprove strongly of the government's 'iron fist' tactics look approvingly upon the young dissidents as keepers of the country's conscience.

Newsweek, 30 May 1988

In a State such as Israel, which places great emphasis on protection of the freedom of expression, journalism provides an especially effective front for a terrorist organization. Journalists have wide access to public and private matters. Therefore, journalists may play a

144

significant role in a terrorist organization by gathering intelligence, disseminating directives, and recruiting new members. Israel's commitment to freedom of expression is demonstrated daily, both within the State and in the administered areas . . . Journalists, however, cannot use their professional status as a shield to insulate themselves from criminal liability for providing vital support to the perpetration of violent acts.

Ministry of Justice, State of Israel, 30 August 1989

It's all right for them to keep Palestinians as political prisoners in jail, but to have Jews – well, it's very embarrassing for them.

Roni Ben Efrat, April 1989

On 23 April 1988 Roni Ben Efrat, a 36-year-old Jewish editor of the biweekly left-wing Hebrew newspaper *Derech Hanitzotz*, was at Ben Gurion Airport about to board a jet for Rome. She was on her way to an anti-fascist rally, but shortly after arriving at the airport and checking in her luggage, she was intercepted by Israeli police. As a left-wing activist Ben Efrat was blacklisted in Israel and always had to go through special procedures; she thought that this time was no different and that she was just being stopped for a routine check.

It was not routine. As she was led to the police room in the airport, she asked the policeman what was happening.

'You're under arrest,' he said drily.

A policewoman stepped in and demanded that Ben Efrat undress, but the policeman interrupted and asked her to follow him. He led her through side stairs to an area underneath the departure terminal, and then into a room with three bunk-beds. Two civilians and another young woman were sitting there waiting.

Ben Efrat asked, 'Who are you?'

'Come on,' one said in an amused tone. 'Do you really not know who we are?'

They told her to sit down, relax, not to worry. One said that if she cooperated, she might even be able to catch her plane. Ben Efrat felt her throat becoming dry, but she concentrated on appearing calm. 'I know I am under arrest,' she told them. 'I won't answer anything.'

Beneath the steady exterior her stomach began to knot with tension. The two women said nothing. Later on, at the Petah Tiqwa detention and interrogation centre, she found that the civilians were two of her leading interrogators.

She had known for about six weeks before the day at the airport that she would be arrested. In February her newspaper *Derech Hanitzotz* was stripped of its licence because of alleged ties with the DFLP (Democratic Front for the Liberation of Palestine), a left-wing branch of the PLO. On 16 February, two days before the licence incident, Ribhi al-Aruri, a former student activist at Birzeit University who edited the Arabic edition of *Derech Hanitzotz*, had been arrested at Roni Ben Efrat's Jerusalem flat and brought to the Military Court in Ramallah in the West Bank. Arrested with him was his brother-in-law Jamal Zakut, a trade union activist from Gaza.

Ben Efrat remembers the night he was arrested because it was like a scene from a film. Not something that could happen to her. She had friends to supper; they were having coffee around eleven o'clock when there was a fierce pounding at the door. She got up; her two children, Jonathan and Ruth, and her friends' children were all asleep.

She called out, 'Who is it?'

They answered, 'Police!'

At the door were plain-clothes policemen and army men; she

remembers thinking that the neighbourhood was full of them. The police showed her an arrest warrant for Jamal Zakut, claiming that he was wanted. They swarmed into the small flat, searching the room and the beds where the children slept, and left shortly after with Jamal and Ribhi. On 8 March Ribhi al-Aruri was given six months' administrative detention (without trial) and he was later adopted by Amnesty International. Jamal Zakut went through months of torture in a Gaza prison before being deported to Lebanon with other Palestinian activists. The remaining *Derech Hanitzotz* journalists – all Jews – were arrested one by one.

One week before Roni Ben Efrat was taken at the airport her ex-husband, Ya'akov, also a *Derech Hanitzotz* editor, had been arrested at his home in an East Jerusalem neighbourhood. Michal Schwartz, a mother of two, was arrested after Roni, on 27 April. The next to go were the literary editor, Hadas Lahav, and her future husband, the publisher of *Derech Hanitzotz*, Assaf Adiv.

On 26 May, after being interrogated by the Shin Bet, the Ben Efrats, Schwartz and Adiv were indicted on a number of security offences against the state of Israel. These included contacting a foreign agent, membership of an illegal organization, meeting a foreign agent (PLO), serving an illegal organization and membership of a terrorist organization. The Israeli court had, essentially, charged them with treason, saying not only that the journalists had become agents of the DFLP, but also that their newspaper was funded by the organization. Ya'akov Ben Efrat was charged with possessing the propaganda material of an illegal organization. Hadas Lahav was released after twelve days of solitary confinement, and claimed that she was 'psychologically' abused by the Shin Bet, that a Palestinian prisoner was brought in before her while she was being interrogated and she was told they would torture him until she talked.

The case attracted national and international attention, largely because the editors were Jews who, in the eyes of the authorities, had greatly wronged and endangered the state of Israel. 'The case is extremely unusual,' reported Joel Brinkley of *The New York Times*, 'because unlike the Arab press, the Israeli press seldom get into trouble.' Despite the fact that the editors were all of the far Left and their newspaper considered extreme, the manner in which the case was handled drew criticism from even the more right-wing papers in Israel. On Wednesday, 11 May 1988, the *Jerusalem Post* published the following leader:

LIFT THAT FOG

Five editorial staff members of the two banned newspapers have since been taken in by the police . . . the suspicions against them are officially said to have nothing to do with their being journalists, and everything with the security of the state. They are said to be suspected of so heinous a connection with terrorist organizations that even consultation with their attorneys was not to be readily granted them.

A thick fog of secrecy is enveloping the entire case. If the authorities do not wish the conclusion to be drawn that the real issue here is not truly state security but the democratic right to air the unpopular ideas considered dangerous by the government, let them promptly lift that fog.

I had heard about the case through Felicia Langer, who had spent most of 1988 defending the Jewish journalists. In April 1989 she sent me to talk to Roni Ben Efrat, who had recently been released from prison and was active in organizing support for her three colleagues serving sentences in solitary confinement. Their demand to be imprisoned with Palestinian political prisoners had continuously been rejected.

Roni was tall and slender; she wore glasses and had a wide, open smile. She had been set free four months earlier, and still looked exhausted. Michal Schwartz and Ya'akov Ben Efrat were in prison, but the office was full of other journalists making photocopies, answering telephones, speaking loudly in Hebrew. Roni sat at a desk near the door, with two telephones and stacks of newspapers in front of her. She got up suddenly and disappeared into a back room, returning with a large cuttings book that a volunteer had kept during the trial; it was crammed with international newspaper articles about the journalists.

'The Shin Bet told us they were going to clear their slandered name on our trial,' Ben Efrat announced. Before their case, she said, the Shin Bet had been involved in criminal acts of covering up and killing prisoners through torture. 'Their reputation was at point zero.' She shut the cuttings book firmly. Someone brought us coffee and she stared into her cup. 'Our case was the silencing of an opposition. A witch hunt.'

Their plight had not gone unnoticed. By April 1989 the journalists had been adopted by Amnesty International as prisoners of conscience. They had become a symbol. To the Left the journalists were an opposition that had been systematically silenced by the government. To the Right they were good Israelis who had gone too far, crossed the border, committed treason. They had broken the rules.

Roni Ben Efrat was born in central Israel, near Tel Aviv, in 1952, the daughter of Scottish émigrés who had come to Israel to live on a kibbutz. Her parents were among the founders of kibbutz Kfar Hanassi in upper Galilee, but left shortly after to found an agricultural village, Kfar Mordechai. As a child she played in the nearby ruins of a Palestinian village, Bashit, swinging from apricot and nut trees, dreaming that she was in a magic forest. Her family was close-knit, her parents were Zionists and supported the Jewish state, but Ben Efrat recalled that they were 'liberal, not fanatic. I don't know if they completely understood what they were doing to the native people. I'm sure they were told a lot of lies. I don't know if they ever talked about who was there before, because no one ever really talked about it.'

As a first-generation Israeli Roni was brought up in a protected, rarefied environment in which she had little contact with Arabs, and yet early on she began to formulate strong humanistic views. The Palestinians who did not leave in the war of 1948 – around 150,000 in number – were confined to their villages under military rule until 1966. 'Like the rest of my generation, we did not see the Arabs until 1967. We were raised on fairy tales. A land without a people to a people without a land.'

For Ben Efrat, the big shock came in 1967, in the aftermath of the Six Day War. Suddenly the owners of the land that Jewish families lived on reappeared. Refugees from the West Bank camps started knocking on Jewish doors. 'They wanted to see their old houses, their old orchards. For many Jews, this was an uncomfortable situation. The guests had arrived to claim their rights,' she said. 'Through the occupation, we revealed the crime that we had managed to cover for nineteen years and the victims of our take-over in 1948 became visible again.'

Unlike her contemporaries, she was unimpressed by the 1967 victory. By the time she was fifteen, shortly after the occupation, she began to feel a nagging sense of disenchantment. 'I was brought up on two myths: one, that Israel was a defenceless country, and two, that we were always under attack. And I was sure, I was absolutely certain, that we Israelis would give back the land that we had conquered.' In the early, heady days of the victory, when Israel was flooded with confidence and camaraderie, she was 'constantly arguing with my teachers and schoolmates'. A few months after the war she visited occupied East Jerusalem with her parents on a holiday. 'I sensed in the Israelis a feeling of the conqueror. And I hated it.'

There were marked changes in Israeli society. The biggest was the emphasis on materialism as the West Bank opened its market and cheap labour streamed into Israel, causing a boom in the economy. 'A new state of *nouveaux riches* started emerging,' she recalled. 'The new, ugly Israeli is something I remember. The good life, the trips abroad, the frenzy of buying things, the frantic building. It went on and on until 1973.' She felt unsettled, resentful, overtly critical. 'But all this was before I became an anti-Zionist.'

At eighteen Ben Efrat left home. She was not feeling particularly patriotic and delayed going into the army. She had no idea what to study, so in 1970 she enrolled at a teacher training college in the Negev Desert. Within months she met Ya'akov Ben Efrat, who would become her husband.

'Ya'akov was very critical,' she remarked. 'He was the first person I had met who spelt out the ugly phenomena of Israeli society.' They began to live together. 'At that time couples did not do that. It just wasn't done.'

They left the Negev for Jerusalem, where they finished their studies at the university. By the time they arrived, the Israeli Left had started to take shape, absorbing values from the European student revolts, and as Ya'akov drifted towards politics, Roni followed him. She read political theory and socialism, books on what Zionism was about. She finished a degree in history and the Bible at the Hebrew University and gave birth to two children, which secured her exemption from the army.

'As I began to read, I began to understand and to grasp that the real injustice of Zionism was what it did to the Palestinians. And to understand that we're not talking about mistakes, but a method. The concept of a state for Jewish people leaves no room for anyone else, not to become part of the Middle East, but to dominate it. A Zionist state does not want to merge, or to become part of another nation. It's a very special kind of colonialism.'

For many women of Ben Efrat's generation, the movement that shaped their lives was feminism. For Roni Ben Efrat, it was politics. When she studied politics, or worked on a project, she felt awakened. All at once the things that had felt so strange when she was a child seemed to make sense: she understood why she argued over history with her Zionist teachers. She understood the deserted apricot trees near her childhood house, the ancient mosque. There were so many things that her parents had never told her, that her teachers refused to explain.

For one thing, there was her past, which was clouded in mystery. 'Suddenly I realized that all our history is an ongoing attempt to extinguish the Palestinians. It's a sad history, because they didn't have a chance – no national awareness, no united front against a fresh British colonialism and this very confusing movement of the Jewish people, Zionism. And they simply did not have the tools to deal with it.'

She began to question the entire Zionist movement. Were the émigrés who arrived in Palestine to form a Jewish state not aware of what they were doing, or was it something far more sinister? When her parents came from Scotland, fresh with ideas of going back to the land and collective living, a new way of life, did they really know?

It is a moot point with many Israelis, a source of guilt and contemplation. How could a group of people who had suffered so much during the Holocaust inflict similar means of abuse on another group of people? 'I don't quite know if the survivors of the Holocaust engage in this,' she said slowly. 'I think the leaders of this state manipulated the helplessness of the Jewish people into the conviction that because of what was done to us, we have the right to do whatever we like to safeguard our existence.

And this kind of position is worked out to the very last detail. Suddenly the way you view the world is upside down, and everyone is against you. You don't say, "The world doesn't like me because I'm an oppressor." You say, "The world doesn't like me because I'm a Jew."

'The Holocaust was used cynically by the Zionist leaders to create a new super Middle East/European power. The Palestinian land, which was defined by the Zionist leaders with such joy as the "miracle", had become the Palestinians' nakbeh, their calamity. The young Israeli democracy was a fake based on the "disappearance" of the Palestinians. Could the Zionist state afford to let the thousands of Palestinians (who were driven to leave during the 1948 war) be first-class citizens of Israel, voting for Israel's parliament? And so, that is how the Palestinian nakbeh opened the door for the Israel democracy myth. A myth based on expelling a people and robbing a land.'

As a mother she began to watch a new generation of Israeli children emerge. It frightened her. 'The attitude of young Israelis is yes, we are occupying land, so what? After 1967 things became more clear, the brutal question of occupation became more legitimate. Children of today are completely insensitive to the suffering of Palestinians. For them to see an Arab cleaning the streets is the most natural vision. For me, it drives me nuts. It goes against my guts.'

Her new-found 'Zionist revelations' were not immediately translated into action. There were years when the focus of Roni and Ya'akov's political group, Hanitzotz, was on Troskyite theory and distant movements for national liberation, like that in Nicaragua. In the early eighties they began to concentrate on Israel.

The first trigger came in 1980, when the Jewish Underground launched its assassination attempt on Palestinian West Bank mayors, including Bassam Shak'ah. Following that a sort of mini-intifada erupted in the occupied territories. Hanitzotz shifted their attentions from global politics to the Israeli–Palestinian conflict. They began studying Arabic and Palestinian politics. They started to view the concept of a Jewish state as essentially racist: 'A state should be for all citizens. Everyone who wants to live here should be able to. There is a set of written and unwritten racist laws – Arabs can't buy land, live in Jewish cities, can't get budgets for anything because they don't serve in the army,' Ben Efrat said. 'All of this makes the Jewish population a privileged population. That is a Jewish state.'

Writing from prison while awaiting his trial, Ya'akov Ben Efrat described the framework and goals of the group:

The Hanitzotz organization operates, most openly, in the framework of the Democratic Front for Peace and Equality (HADASH) in cooperation with the Communist Party of Israel. The goal of this group is to bring an end to Israeli occupation of the territories and to recognize the PLO as sole legitimate representative of the Palestinian people, as a step towards establishing a stable peace by means of an international convention for peace in the Middle East.

At the same time the organization works for a fundamental, democratic change of regime in Israel, so that Jews and Arabs enjoy equal rights, through the abrogation of all forms of discrimination and racism currently enforced by the most wide-ranging legislation.

On 4 June 1982 Israel invaded Lebanon in an attempt to crush the PLO infrastructure there. It was a difficult time for Israel domestically; whereas the wars of 1967 and 1973 had been met with a huge amount of support, the invasion of Lebanon struck a note of discontent among even the conservative politicians. There was an enormous outcry from the public at large. Suddenly more and more soldiers were refusing to serve in Lebanon or in the occupied territories. 'It was step two,' Ben Efrat said, 'Israel becoming a military state. You watch Israel becoming a strategic monster which sees itself having a role in the world.'

Ben Efrat thought the war with Lebanon was when the Israeli Peace Camp began to gain momentum. 'It was the turning-point . . . it was the first time that I understood fully how the Israeli government wanted to finish off the Palestinian problem in a military way. All the things we see today in the intifada, we've seen already. It was a dress rehearsal. By June they invaded Lebanon, by July Ansar, the first huge "concentration camp" for Palestinians and Lebanese, was erected.' (In the spring of 1988 a similar camp was built for prisoners of the intifada in the Negev, also known as Ketziot.)

When reports of the Palestinian massacres at the Sabra and Shatila refugee camps began to filter through (in which Red Cross officials estimate between eight hundred and one thousand Palestinians were killed by Phalangists in an attack underhandedly orchestrated by Israel), even more soldiers refused to go to Lebanon, and the Yesh Gvul, the movement of soldiers who would not serve, grew. The war in Lebanon, in a sense, solidified the Israeli Peace Camp.

The early eighties for the Hanitzotz members were spent developing contacts in the West Bank and Gaza and studying the Palestinian national liberation movement. 'As left people we naturally felt closer to the ideology and politics of the left factions of the PLO. This had nothing to do with our being a faction of any Palestinian organization.'

Yet a report issued by the state of Israel's Ministry of Justice on 30 August 1989 stated the contrary:

In the early 1980's, three of the Four contacted representatives of the Democratic Front for the Liberation of Palestine ('DFLP'); the fourth, Roni Ben Efrat, joined the meetings some time later. Under Israel law, the DFLP is a terrorist organization. It is one of the most extreme factions of the Palestine Liberation Organization ('PLO'), and is headed by Na'if Hawatmeh, the internationally notorious terrorist. Initial meetings with the Four were conducted by Sallah Rafat, who is a member of the DFLP's political wing, a member of the PLO's Central Council, and commander of the DFLP's armed attacks in the administered areas and Israel. In subsequent contacts, the Four met with top DFLP representatives including Hikmat al-Sabri (first secretary of the PLO in Greece, who orchestrated DFLP activities in the administered areas), and internationally known terrorists Hani Issawi and Mohammed Labadi. The Four received regular financial support from these contacts.

As a result of the meetings, the Four became members of the DFLP and under its direction and with its financing began to publish a Hebrew language newspaper called *Derech Hanitzotz*.

The intifada officially began in December 1987. For Roni Ben Efrat and Hanitzotz, its effect was 'thrilling. It had an immense power, even for the Jewish people who were not political. It was an immensely popular outburst of power and energy and unity, and it put out good things for the struggle. And I guess it was a big relief for people like us who were struggling against the occupation and for Palestinians.' She paused. 'Of course, more so for the Palestinians, because they had been so oppressed. Suddenly, seeing that you have the power to change things, you have this sense of relief. After being repressed and hopeless for so long, you realize the army is afraid of you! This was new. Before, any jeep could pass safely through an Arab village. Now there was graffiti, Palestinian flags – all this was so new.'

She was down in Gaza, covering a story at the Shifa Hospital, when she looked up and saw a Palestinian flag on the wall for the first time. She stared and her heart 'began to beat like mad', because in thirty-five years of living in Israel she had never seen the flag hanging before. To Ben Efrat it was an indication that things were going to change, that the Palestinians were going to take no more.

The first six months of the intifada were frantic, full of demonstrations, riots, funerals, clashes, conferences. The office was packed with journalists and Ben Efrat felt as though she were caught up in a historical opportunity. 'You had to work hard to sustain it. The force of the intifada cannot go on for ever, and we felt that we were living in a special point in time. You couldn't put it off.'

Their office was in Korresh Street, and they often worked through the night. They decided to turn the biweekly Arab edition of their newspaper into a weekly and increase the distribution from three thousand to five thousand copies. 'We had some influence,' Ben Efrat said. 'And the authorities saw it.'

They also had contacts. They were accused by more conservative Israelis of 'becoming Palestinian' and crossing the border. 'Our struggle was, and is, making Israel a democracy. That means that we have to deal with people inside Israel – to change attitudes. Our society has to cure itself by ending the occupation. Only then will it begin to heal itself from all the sickness that comes from being an occupier.'

Others did not see her work as a struggle, or as 'healing' society. The authorities saw it as dangerous.

And so she was arrested. From the airport that day in April Roni Ben Efrat was taken to the Petah Tiqwa detention and interrogation centre and later transferred to the detention centre at the Russian Compound prison in Jerusalem. She did not see a lawyer for fifteen days. On 29 May, along with Michal Schwartz, Ben Efrat was moved to Neve Tirza, a prison for women in Ramla, near Tel Aviv. The women asked to be placed with other political prisoners rather than criminals. The request was rejected.

Ben Efrat had begun to write to her children in the form of a journal. It was a way of keeping her sanity, and also of keeping in touch with Jonathan and Ruth. She was worried about them, about their being alone and what they would suffer because she and Ya'akov (from whom she had been separated for some time) were activists. 'Since you were little, and even more when you grew up a bit,' she wrote to them, 'you have accompanied me and borne along with me all the difficulties of the political path I have chosen. For entire Saturdays you stayed at home until I returned from subscription drives or rallies and you never forgot to turn on the water heater without my asking.'

She was deeply frightened of being in prison. She and Michal heard before they arrived at Neve Tirza that someone had begun to incite the criminal prisoners. They were apparently waiting 'to take the law into their own hands'.

'Along with the trial, which we will go through in the District Court in Jerusalem,' Ben Efrat wrote in her journal, 'there will be another battle, no less fascinating and fateful, the battle for our lives in prison, for fulfilling our demand to spend the imprisonment with the Palestinian political prisoners.'

The day of her transfer to Neve Tirza was hot. As her car reached the gate of the prison, it stopped briefly: ahead was another car with several prisoners waiting to be taken for medical treatment. At the sight of the journalists the prisoners began to jeer, '*Derech Hanitzotz* have arrived, Arab fuckers, traitors, commit suicide. You'll see what will happen to you here!' The driver in Ben Efrat's car appeared to have heard and understood what the prisoners said, but continued to stare straight ahead and did nothing. A female police officer approached the car slowly, looked down at their belongings and leaned her head inside the car. 'What's this!' she shouted. 'Did you bring your entire homes?'

Inside the prison the three women were supplied with toothbrushes, a scarred plastic old-fashioned cup, a packet of 'wartime' sanitary towels, bedding and clothing. Ben Efrat, who is tall and long-limbed, was given trousers for a much smaller woman. 'Although my size is obvious,' she wrote in her journal, 'she brought size thirty-six trousers. She did her best to humiliate me.' She was given red, white and blue clownish shoes. She sat down to try them on.

Lunch was an ordeal. The whole prison was put under emergency regime. Men were brought in to make order. The prison manager, Chaya Shoham, had to explain to the journalists what was happening: apparently the prisoners had seen the television news with the Hanitzotz prisoners going to prison giving the V-for-victory sign.

Roni and Michal were marched through the dining hall to an empty room belonging to two criminal prisoners who were already in the hall eating. Soon other prisoners appeared at the door, one by one, throwing bowls of soup or oranges through the peep-hole and cursing at them. Occasionally political prisoners passed by and whispered words of encouragement: 'Be strong, we are with you.' But within minutes of arriving 'the door suddenly opened and our "room-mate" attacked me like a tiger released from a cage. She twisted my left arm . . . I began shouting at her and Michal grabbed her from behind . . . we tried to calm her down. We told her that we, also, were interested in getting out. Shouts of encouragement to her continued to be heard through the peep-hole. It was obvious that she was proud of being able to carry out her mission well.

'After she calmed down a bit, she wanted to know how we could have "purchased bombs for the PLO in order to kill children". We explained what we were really accused of and she admitted in fact that she had not read any newspaper. We understood that someone was hard at work behind the scenes in order to inflame the atmosphere.'

Shortly after the encounter Schwartz and Ben Efrat were transferred to a room for political prisoners, but 'in the evening hours curses were heard from the criminal prisoners' cells and the shouts "Traitors!" "Death Penalty!" "Fucking with Arabs! You won't leave this place alive."'

By the end of May Roni and Michal had been moved to a 'separation wing' in another fenced-in building. They were put in a better cell (2.5 by 3 metres), with a shower, a toilet and two bunk-beds.

The days passed and the real turning-point came one night when a curious, hesitant voice was heard: 'Why do you betray the Jews?'

'We started speaking to her and explaining who and what we were. We explained that we were charged with publishing a paper funded by the PLO, not bombs and weapons. That there had been incitement against us. That we opposed the occupation and supported the withdrawal from the territories.'

After that the atmosphere altered radically. There were no more threats and no more shouts, and no more buckets of yoghurt mixed with urine and cigarette butts were thrown into their cell. 'The following morning the girls passed by our room in order to demonstrate to us that their attitude had changed. Suddenly we saw the faces behind the curses and shouts and they stopped being threatening.'

Roni Ben Efrat and Michal Schwartz remained in the separation wing for eight weeks. Following a five-day hunger strike they were given a separate room in the general wing of the prison. They studied Arabic, testing each other on vocabulary.

They read. They slept. Roni kept her diaries. In June an initial attempt by Felicia Langer to release Ben Efrat from prison was overruled by the Supreme Court. The trial officially began on 8 September 1988 before the Jerusalem District Court.

Hadas Lahav was summoned to testify for the prosecution, but refused and was jailed for contempt of court. At the second session she was produced from jail to testify, and again refused. The court then released her, but ruled to accept as evidence her confession made earlier in the year. The trial dragged on throughout the autumn when a prisoner, who had been planted by the Shin Bet to gain evidence against *Derech Hanitzotz* editors, took the stand.

It was a low point for the journalists. The Shin Bet 'agent', Ezri Shomil, a convict who was serving time for burglary, told the court that he had agreed to help the state because he had read in the newspapers that the editors were traitors. 'I worked for the Shin Bet because I love the country,' he said. His main function, the court was told, was to deliver newspapers and letters to and from the editors, many of them written on napkins.

In January 1989 Felicia Langer decided with her clients to end the trial by plea bargaining, eliminating the severe charge of contact with a foreign agent, but leaving the charge of membership of a hostile organization. Ben Efrat was released from prison the same day; Michal Schwartz remained for another ten months, until the end of October 1989. Ya'akov was held for a total of thirty months, Assaf for eighteen. Until the end the prison administration refused to allow them to be among the political prisoners.

Two years after our first meeting Roni cooked me dinner in her small flat in a large block in San Martine, West Jerusalem. Her life, after prison, had continued in much the same way as it had before. She worked for *Challenge*, a magazine published by Hanitzotz, was still deeply committed and rarely considered the fact that she had lost nearly a year of her life. She said that prison made her 'stronger'.

The political group worked and socialized together. Ya'akov Ben Efrat and Michal Schwartz had married. When I arrived at Roni's flat, it was full of people – Hadas Lahav and her husband, Assaf Adiv, were there with their new baby, who was crawling on a sofa. Roni was on the telephone, and a tape of the Gypsy Kings was playing. She was making our dinner, she informed me, chicken and vegetables in a slow cooker: 'Working girl's food,' she called out, cupping her hand over the phone.

After the others had left, we ate our meal in silence, listening to the music. She made strong coffee. I asked her, tentatively, if there was any part of her life that she regretted: the year in prison, the fact that she will always be watched by the authorities, the all-consuming commitment to 'the struggle'.

She shook her head slowly. 'I could not imagine not doing this work, ever.'

Some time later I found a book in a shop in San Francisco, a collection of interviews with the Israeli Peace Camp; among them was one with Roni. When asked what kept her going, Roni Ben Efrat replied:

What keeps me going? I think it's the fact that I simply wouldn't be able to get up in the morning and look at myself in the mirror without doing the things that I'm doing. I'm serious about it. Living so close to the atrocities and the injustice that is being practised against Palestinians, it makes me feel that I don't have the right to be here if I am not doing something to change it. I think this is what is motivating me.

Sometimes I ask myself, if there were to be a Palestinian state – if this problem were to be solved – then what would happen? I'm just leaving this question open . . .

I met a man near the Jaffa Gate, a Palestinian who had served twenty-three years in prison for planting a bomb near the walls of the Old City. 'I was very young,' he said. 'And it was a long time ago.' He was carrying a beautiful baby in his arms; he was married now and was trying to piece together his life. 'You lose something very deep when you are in prison for such a long time.' He told me how old he was and I worked out that he had been about fifteen when he went to prison: more than half of his life had been spent in a cell.

I said I was writing about the Israeli Left. He put his finger on his lip as though he were deep in thought and advised me to go to the Alternative Information Centre, which collected and disseminated information from the occupied territories and within Israel. I was to speak to someone called Mikado Warschawski, who was married to the lawyer Leah Tsemel. He had been a comrade of the Hanitzotz group in the 1970s and had been arrested and imprisoned under the Prevention of Terror Ordinance. As director of the Alternative Information Centre he was often accused of being extreme, radical and 'on the border': essentially a Jew who had abandoned his roots and become Palestinian.

I waited in the centre's office, in the same depressing Korresh Street building where Langer had worked and Roni Ben Efrat still did, and read a newsletter called *News From Within*. On the bottom, next to the copyright, the words 'anti-copyright, 1989' were written in fine print. There was a photograph of Mikado being taken away after his trial and several articles about him:

And indeed, he has stood, and still stands, on the border between the Israeli and Palestinian people, with a definite decision to remain among his people, but as close as possible to the other; and on the border of the law, with a decision not to cross it ... the heavy punishment imposed on Warschawski is meant to be a deterrent – that is a warning aimed at the Israeli peace forces not to come close to the border of Israel–Palestinian cooperation.

Mikado came out as I was reading it. He looked at me curiously. He made some Nescafé, picked up a packet of French cigarettes from a desk and led me to a tiny windowless office in the back. He did not say a word until I began. 'Where were you born? When did you come to Israel?'

He spoke English with a heavy French accent and chainsmoked, lighting fresh cigarettes from the old ones. He came from Strasburg, he said, from an orthodox Jewish family. His father was the chief rabbi and had served in the French resistance during the Second World War. 'I was brought up with strong anti-racist values and my first concept of the occupation here was linked to the Nazi occupation of France.' At sixteen he was sent to Talmudic school in Jerusalem, 'but I did not receive a Zionist education'. When the war broke out in 1967, he remembers the time 'in which everyone became part of a big, big history. It was a short and tremendous war and the victory festival lasted three or four years. But very quickly I was confronted with the issue of occupation.'

His first crisis came at the end of 1967. 'It was not just the occupation, but the ideology behind it of being omnipotent. And the Arabs were nothing.' He decided to begin working with left-wing organizations shortly after the war, first by publishing anti-government poetry. Later, in 1984, he banded with other left-wing groups and opened the Alternative Information Centre in the wake of the Lebanon war as a sort of focus for mass opposition; it was a time, he said, when Israeli media and the international press were very poor in giving facts and information about the occupied territories – repression, resistance, trials, prisons. 'After the war in Lebanon the national unity was broken. Things that were happening and not becoming known needed a place where people could go to find out.'

In February 1987 the centre was closed by a military order. Mikado believed that the decision was taken at a very high level; all equipment and archive materials were seized and staff were arrested on suspicion of links with terrorist organizations. After forty-eight hours everyone except Mikado, who was being held in the Russian Compound prison in Jerusalem and inter-rogated by the Shin Bet, was released. 'There was no violence,' he said. 'But that total isolation, that small dirty cell, that feeling that you are cut off from the world, not knowing whether it was day or night.' He stubbed out his cigarette with force and lit another.

During the interrogation Mikado was told, 'You have been active for almost twenty years with quite radical political views. And except for a few harassments, you have been free to do whatever you wanted. Isn't that true?' He replied that it was more or less true. The interrogator went on, 'And do you know why? Because we are living in democracy. And democracy protects people's rights to express whatever they want, including people like you, with radical, anti-Zionist political positions.' He asked Mikado if he agreed, and Mikado again answered, yes, more or less. The interrogation continued. 'But there,' he said, and pointed in an eastern direction, towards the West Bank, 'there is no democracy. There is occupation. And we have a problem with you guys and your centre. It's not clear whether it's in Israel or in the occupied territories.'

Mikado was questioned about alleged meetings with leaders of the PFLP (Popular Front for the Liberation of Palestine) in Cyprus. He was later charged with supporting a terrorist organization and giving typesetting services to various illegal organizations. His wife represented him in court and by November 1989 he had been acquitted of most of the charges, but as director of the centre, he was convicted of typesetting a booklet attributed to the PFLP, which documented torture and interrogation procedures of the Shin Bet. Mikado claimed that he did not know the booklet belonged to the PFLP and that he was simply involved in typesetting a leaflet; he refused to identify the person who brought it to him. For 'closing his eyes' he was sentenced to twenty months in prison. The centre was fined ten thousand shekels.

His sentence was reduced to eight months. Two years later he had reopened the centre. They were still printing 'underground' newsletters, organizing protests, resisting the occupation. He gave me a pile of old newsletters and left the room. When he came back, there was a woman accompanying him, a handsome woman in her fifties with a straight dark bob that hung over her eyes. She smiled and held out her hand; her voice was throaty. She made a cup of coffee and led me to her office, across from Mikado's.

Tikva Parnas Honig is part of the Women's Network, something she describes as a more 'centred' left organization, and the Women Who Support Political Prisoners. She told me she was sixty-three, a different generation from that of Roni Ben Efrat and Mikado. Her generation is the one that helped found the state of Israel, and Tikva had fought in the War of Independence as a young girl.

In 1948, when the war broke out, she was studying at the Hebrew University on Mount Scopus. One day she was listening to the radio with her friends and suddenly felt as though she had to do something. She went out and found a recruiting office and enlisted in Palmach, an élite unit of the Jewish forces, as a wireless operator.

'I was a different person altogether then,' she said slowly, staring out of the window. 'Nationalistic, Zionistic. I never questioned the role of Zionism and I never saw contradictions in establishing an independent state in Palestine. I never realized what we were uprooting. For my generation, Palestinians were simply a kind of harassment.'

Tikva was born in Australia and came to what was then Palestine with her family when she was three years old. Her mother was a fifth-generation Galilee Sephardic Jew; her father owned orange groves near Beit Kerin, between Tel Aviv and Haifa. Every day on her way to school she saw Palestinian workers selling fruits and vegetables, but she never acknowledged them. 'I was part of this brainwashing that was so self-righteous. To buy only Jewish products, to redeem the land. At that time we were not supposed even to hire Arab workers. But my father did not keep that law, until the authorities found out and made him keep it.'

She recalled one day in particular, when she went to visit an Arab worker who had been fired from his job. What she saw disturbed her. 'He lived in a tent in the orange groves. There was a baby in a hammock. I remember thinking, this cannot be right. But my generation did not ask questions. We did not deal with the root of the conflict. The conflict, we thought, had to do with borders. Not with the fact that the whole Jewish colonization movement had uprooted the Palestinians.' Although she had doubts, she was still, essentially, a Zionist. 'But then I began to read Marx. I began to realize that I was the victim of a long process of dehumanizing the Palestinians.'

At eighteen and a half she left for university. 'I shared a room with an Israeli friend. We both thought we were progressive, but when the war broke out, we asked each other, could you shoot an Arab? And we both came to the conclusion that if the Arabs were wearing European clothes, we could not. But if they were wearing a keffiyeh and Arab clothes, then we could.'

When she joined the Palmach, she felt that she was doing something grand for her country, something on an enormous scale. She was defending the Jewish state. But there were nagging worries. 'I remember sitting down and writing a letter to my parents on 30 October 1948 on stationery taken from an Arab petrol station that we had confiscated. I was writing on someone else's stationery and I didn't even refer to it! I was so shocked when I found that letter recently.

'I described to my parents the conquest of an Arab village, and how we felt when we did it, and the hundreds of Palestinians we met on the way and how they were starving to death and begging to come back to their villages. And there were two Jewish-American volunteers who were shouting, "If this new state can't take care of its citizens, it should not have been started." I recall I was so annoyed at that time with the American Jews who kept shouting that we had to look after their people. I wrote: "Dear Mother and Father, I am so sick of these philanthropic American Zionists." I just did not relate to what I was doing, because I thought what I was doing was for the good of Israel.'

Now she works with political prisoners and women's groups, and sees the basic violation of human rights buried deep in the history and the traditions of Israel. 'It is not just a question of borders. The state of Israel takes away the rights of twenty per cent of the people within Israel, that is, Palestinians who live within the green line. When the state discriminates against non-Jews, there is no prospect of democracy.

'You see, that is the problem with Israel today. We always think of what is for the good of the state. Even if you get a progressive journalist speaking out on torture, he does not do it for practical reasons. Even if you find liberal attitudes towards the Palestinians, you find, "What is good for the Israeli state?" Once it is based on these conditions, it's bound to fail – because other options are there. And they are deep-rooted, part of the system, part of the history.

'Without changing the basis of the Jewish state, with its explicit aims, and the attitudes of what it is built on – that is, we need a big state for a big *aliya* [Jewish immigration to Israel] – nothing will change. Not even the intifada will change things.' She smiled wanly, lit a cigarette and repeated herself. 'Not even the intifada will change things.'

If people like Roni Ben Efrat and Mikado and Tikva are called the dreaming Left, what is it they dream about? Coexistence? Two states? A life without blue licence plates, yellow licence plates, green lines, identification cards? Or, even more abstractly, that notion of peace?

Very rarely did I come across an apathetic Israeli, an Israeli with little or nothing to say about the political situation. 'If you have three Jews,' someone told me, 'you have four opinions.' I wanted the opinion of someone who was moderately left, not extreme, not radical, someone who served in the army, who was not happy with the situation, but who still felt like an Israeli. I met Benni Burger, who was then the executive director of B'tselem, the Israeli human rights lobby. He had worked on human rights issues, but was not considered far left. A friend of his said he was very interesting on the subject of 'Jewish morality, the question of occupier and the occupied, and Israeli guilt'.

Twice a year Benni Burger served his army reserve duty; yet he was against human rights abuse. He did not agree with left-wing radicalism, such as some of the work of Felicia Langer. He said her ideas were 'too extreme'. His concerns were that his

Israeli society was crumbling, 'deteriorating from within'. It was exactly the sort of attitude that Tikva disagreed with.

Burger was a first-generation Israeli, the son of a Belgian jazz musician. He had lost two grandmothers and two grandfathers in Auschwitz and his mother had been incarcerated in Buchenwald. When he was a child, he said he always felt the lingering shadow of the Holocaust. There was something more cynical, tougher in him than in the others whom I had met. 'But I am an optimist,' he said when I told him that. 'I spend my days documenting human rights abuse to present it to Israeli society so that in ten years' time they cannot say they did not know what had happened.'

I met him inside a café in Tel Aviv on a hot day in May; he was drinking a double espresso and wearing sunglasses. When I explained I wanted to talk about this abstract thing, Jewish morality, he laughed.

'Israel is not the classic occupier,' he said. 'We were always the oppressed and the Jews have always been pragmatic. Pragmatism is the middle name of every Jew in the world. Jews always accepted what they became. They never had this Arab disease called honour.

'What goes on in the mind of every Israeli is the Holocaust, even if they cannot address it, even if they are not the direct survivors.' He called it the 'demon' in their minds. 'The Holocaust is enough to leave its traces. Not only on the survivors. On their children, and their children's children. Two things happen: you believe that you will never do to others what was done to you. The second is that you don't trust anybody. You are paranoid for security. It's quite normal, especially after the Holocaust when you live among Arabs who say they want to throw you into the sea.'

I told him about being in Aida camp, near Hebron, where I

met Samia, a 33-year-old woman who had spent five years in prison for planting a bomb in Jerusalem. She had been sentenced to thirteen years, but was released in a prisoner exchange. Samia wore a T-shirt that said 'Black Sunday', recalling the Palestinian labourers who had been killed by Jewish settlers near Rishon Lezion. 'But I never wear it outside, where the soldiers can see me,' she said. 'I wear it at home, to remind myself.' Samia said she was officially in mourning: her 24-year-old sister, Amal, had been killed in 1990 on a suicide mission in West Jerusalem. Amal had gone to the Jewish market wearing an exploding belt, with instructions to plant it in a lavatory. Something went wrong and she blew herself up when she went in to remove the belt.

I sat on a garish, flowered couch next to her and took notes. 'She was going to plant the bomb in the Jewish market and try to blow it up?'

Samia nodded.

I said, 'But I go to that market, and I'm not Jewish. So do a lot of Jewish people who are not directly involved in the occupation, or Jews who try to end the occupation. Left-wing Jews. Children. Why would you try to attack innocent people?'

'What do you expect us to do,' Samia said, 'when we are living in this situation? We are dead all the time, even when we are sleeping. It's an operation of sacrifice. Sometimes you have to sacrifice something for the cause. Sometimes it's people who are not involved. It is a revolution, and people win or people die. It's just the way it is.'

Burger listened carefully to that story. 'Eventually we will need a kind of explosion to see that we have to end this,' he said. 'This process will be a public decision, but it will have nothing to do with political leaders. I told you before, I tell you again, we do not want to have a situation here whereby in ten years' time we are forced to say, "I didn't know." Our main *raison d'être* is for our sake – for Israel's sake, not for Palestine. Because the main damage is to Israelis, not to Palestinians. They will have their state, and one day the occupation will be a myth. But it is weakening Israeli society.'

In 1987 Benni Burger, who was then working on a local Israeli news magazine *Koteret Rashit*, commissioned the writer David Grossman to spend seven weeks travelling through the West Bank. An entire issue of the magazine was devoted to Grossman's observations and the final result was his book *The Yellow Wind*. After leaving Burger, I stopped off and bought the book in a West Jerusalem bookshop. At the end Grossman concludes that before he began to write the book,

I could not understand how an entire nation like mine, an enlightened nation by all accounts, is able to train itself to live as a conqueror without making its own life wretched. What happened to us? How were they able to pass their values on to me during those years?

And so I became an artist of sublimation. I found myself developing the same voluntary suspension of questions about ethics and occupation. I did not visit the territories; I did not even go to Old Jerusalem. Because I felt the hatred of the people there, but mostly because I cannot tolerate relations that are not on an equal basis. Like so many others, I began to think of that kidney-shaped expanse of land, the West Bank, as an organ transplanted into my body against my wishes, and about which soon, when I had time, I would come to some sort of conclusion and decision. Of course, that transplanted organ continued to produce antibodies in my consciousness. I also knew how to declaim the familiar words meant to satisfy old sphinxes: it cannot go on this way, the occupation corrupts us, we have created a system of masters and slaves, and so on. But the furnace which forged those words went out and cooled long ago, and I did not want to feel it.

*

The polar opposites of the dreaming Left are the settlers. These are not the young, urban settlers, the yuppies who are attracted by the government's heavy housing subsidies and want to live within commuting distance of Tel Aviv, or even the settlers who argue that the settlements act as security buffers along the valley of the river Jordan or around Jerusalem. The real polar opposites of the Left are the Jews who believe that the land is historically theirs, that the Jewish roots are far too deep ever to give up. When they dream, they dream of tiny little dots that they call towns and that the Palestinians and the Left call settlements, and they dream of those black dots covering the map of what they call Eretz Israel.

The dots are getting closer. There are 151 settlements (132 in the West bank and 19 in Gaza), and the population of most of them has nearly doubled since the intifada began. It is estimated that sixty-five per cent of the West Bank is in Jewish hands. Settlers do not believe that their land will be returned as part of a Middle East peace agreement because they do not acknowledge that the Palestinians' land ever belonged to them. They say that the land has always belonged to the Jews.

Peter Mansfield, however, in his book *The Arabs*, has a different historical perspective:

Who were the inhabitants of the Holy Land at this time [1917]? The Ottoman Empire had no vital statistics for its provinces but it is thought that before the 1914–1918 war, there were about 600,000 Arabs, Muslims and Christians, and about 80,000 Jews. The Jewish population fell during the war as some left, as refugees, under American and other auspices, and a British census of 1918 gave an estimate of 700,000 Arabs and 56,000 Jews. It is therefore quite understandable that the Arabs, who formed at least 90 per cent of the population, should have resented the Balfour Declaration's reference to them as 'the existing non-Jewish communities in Palestine'. Although they were the descendants of a people who had lived in Palestine for at least a thousand years, this phrase appeared to classify them as intruders. As elsewhere in Syria, the Palestinians had an educated upper class who enjoyed considerable privileges under the Turks and held high posts under their administration.

Lord Curzon, who succeeded Balfour as foreign secretary, was also concerned with the plight of the Palestinians after the Balfour Declaration was drawn up. He wrote:

What is to become of the people of this country [Palestine] assuming the Turk to be expelled and the inhabitants not to have been exterminated by the war? There are over half a million of these Syrian Arabs – a mixed community with Arab, Hebrew, Canaanite, Greek, Egyptian and possibly Crusader blood. They and their forefathers have occupied the country for the best part of 1,500 years. They own the soil, which belongs either to the individual landowners or to village communities. They profess the Mohammedan faith. They will not be content either to be expropriated for Jewish immigrants, or to act merely as hewers of wood and drawers of water to the latter.

But the Palestinians were expropriated. Their land was confiscated – largely because of the land ownership system which came about under Ottoman, British and Jordanian rule. There was little or no need for documentation. Land was passed on through the generations; the present society required nothing more official than that. But Israeli law does not recognize their informal system of land ownership. The first settlers in the West Bank arrived as squatters and refused to go. Now the settlements are overwhelming.

Thomas Friedman in *From Beirut to Jerusalem* writes of the expanse of settlements:

once Labor agreed to annex the Old City of Jerusalem and the Temple Mount immediately after the war, fusing modern Israel with the very core of its biblical past, it set a precedent for other biblically inspired settlements throughout the West Bank. It was only a matter of time before these settlements would mushroom everywhere.

The first settler I met was a converted Jew from Chicago called Ed. This was at Kiryat Arba, near Hebron, the earliest settlement in the West Bank, founded shortly after rabbis Moshe Levinger and Eliezer Waldman rented the Arab-owned Park Hotel in April 1968 during the Passover holiday and refused to leave. Hebron was the town, they said, where the patriarchs Abraham, Isaac and Jacob were buried and where Abraham, the father of the nation, purchased his first piece of land in Palestine. This was their land. The settlers first stayed in a military camp and later, with the backing of the Israeli Labour Party, built Kiryat Arba.

In December 1987, the start of the intifada, there were 3,700 residents at Kiryat Arba; four years later, in May 1991, there were 5,500. Kiryat Arba inhabitants have an attitude not dissimilar to that of the pioneers of the Wild West. They see themselves as living on a frontier, having to tame the natives. They see their lives as the ultimate challenge, and consider it their responsibility, as Jews, to reclaim the land.

Kiryat Arba seems to breed extremes. This is the place where ultra-right-wing leader of the Kach Party Meir Kahane lived for a while, and where the Jewish Underground was masterminded.

I had never seen anything quite like it, and I had never come across anyone quite like Ed before either. On the telephone, when I arranged to meet him, he sounded cheerful and gave me instructions about what to do when I drove through the barbed-wire fence that separates the Jewish settlers from the road where the Palestinians walk on their way to their villages or camps. I had a rented West Bank car, I told Ed with some apprehension.

Would that be a problem? Ed whistled under his breath and said he would inform someone at the gate that I was coming in a blue-plated car.

I visited Ed at night, driving slowly through Bethlehem, through Beit Sahour, through the hills as the sky deepened to black. Ed had advised me to follow the signs carefully and to be cautious: 'The Arabs are tossing rocks the size of boulders.' I missed the turning to Kiryat Arba, and finally came to the gates where an armed civilian waved me through. Inside, the settlement was like another world. There was a garishly lit petrol station, a restaurant and a convenience store. Everything seemed to be made of pale stone and fencing; it was grim and depressing. The women wore long skirts with knee socks and kerchiefs tied under their chins. The men had beards and guns.

I pulled into the petrol station to wait for Ed. The attendant looked at my car, gaped and bolted inside the hut. I waited for ten minutes, but Ed did not appear. I locked the car and went into the hut to ask directions to his flat. The attendant stared at me, horrified. He pointed at the car, gesticulating wildly. A small crowd was gathering.

'I'm not an Arab. Can you please tell me how to find –'

One of the women, who spoke English, said, 'You have identification?'

I laid two press cards (one British, one Israeli) and my passport neatly on the table, and the woman and the petrol attendant examined them closely and still shook their heads.

'Please, you go now,' she said finally.

'I have an appointment,' I said.

She shouted, 'Move your car away.' I got into the car and started the engine. Two women passed by and when I tried to talk to them, they shook their heads at me.

Ed turned up. He was a giant. He wore Levis and a checked

shirt, carried a gun in a holster and had a ginger beard that reached his collar. He pumped my hand and apologized. 'They get a little nervous here,' he explained, and pointed at the car. 'They thought you had a bomb in it. You should have brought ID.'

'I did,' I said.

Ed shrugged his enormous shoulders. 'Life in wartime . . .' he said, and drove me in his car to his flat.

His apartment block was a depressing warren of dirty hallways and what appeared to be shoddily constructed buildings. Ed's flat was equally grim and disorganized, with hardly any furniture at all. From the kitchen a pale, blonde woman appeared, considerably younger than Ed, and fled into another room the minute she saw me. There were several small children who gaped at me and did not smile when I said, 'Shalom.'

'Are those all your children?' I asked. I tried to count them.

'Yeah.' Ed said something to them in Hebrew, causing them to scatter in various directions. 'We'll be out here,' he shouted to the silent wife, and led me on to a patio overlooking Kiryat Arba.

Ed was from somewhere in the Midwest of America, a Vietnam veteran. He called Palestinians 'Arabs' and said that before the intifada he used to sit and have a coffee with the Arabs in Hebron. 'Now, no way,' he said. He talked about the world in terms of black and white: Jews and non-Jews. He enlightened me on anti-Semitism and Jew-bashing and protecting oneself. 'It's a war zone out there,' he said, pointing his gun. He talked about the pioneering spirit and 'rebuilding our country from within' and quoted the Torah at length. He talked about David, commander of Israel's mightiest army, establishing his first kingdom in Hebron. He talked about the universal conspiracy against Jews. He said he did not acknowledge the

Palestinians in his country. He said all this with a heavy American accent.

When I suggested, casually, that surely there was not a worldwide conspiracy against Jews, he said he would show me something I would never forget. He was going to take me into the Old City of Hebron, a heavily populated Arab area, to see the Jewish cemetery that had been desecrated. We could not decide whose car to take to drive into the Arab area; mine with the blue plates or his with the yellow. In the end we got into his car and drove to the cemetery. It was nearly ten o'clock, and it was a dark night. I was not sure which made me more uneasy: going to a Jewish cemetery in the middle of an Arab town late at night in a Jewish car, or being anywhere with a slightly crazed settler with a gun.

'Maybe if we're lucky, we'll get hit with a rock or two,' he said cheerfully, manoeuvring the car over a roadblock. 'Then we could have some fun. Just kidding!'

I said, rather weakly, that we did not have to go inside. 'We can look from the gates.'

'No, no, you have to see the swastikas that these people painted. Unbelievable, some Arabs. No respect for anyone.'

Ed turned to me. 'Don't worry, no one will hurt us with this here.' He patted his gun.

It was cold and silent inside the cemetery. He wanted to walk around and inspect each one of the graves that had been spray-painted with graffiti, with intifada slogans. Some had been partially dug up, the earth pushed to one side of the tombstones.

I shivered, but Ed would not let me go until I inspected every gravestone. When we got back into the car and he drove me down the hill to Hebron, he was quiet. Finally, approaching the entrance to the settlement, he spoke: 'Can you believe the world we live in?' he said, shaking his enormous head. 'Crazy, just crazy.'

Some time later I met another Kiryat Arba resident. Before my appointment with Gary Cooperburg ('Yes, that's my real name') from the South Bronx, now an Israeli, I read the pamphlet that I had picked up in Kiryat Arba's yeshiva.

Soldiers, scholars and pioneers . . . rebuilding our country from within! . . . the miraculous return of Judaea and Samaria to the Jewish people in the Six Day War stunned even our own leaders! In 1968 a handful of Jewish pioneers established a yeshiva in the holy city of Hebron, whose yeshiva and Jewish community had been destroyed by the Arab riots in 1929. This yeshiva became the core of the first urban settlement in Judaea and Samaria, Kiryat Arba. Soon, other settlements were established in the Hebron area and the Jews returned to the heart of the city.
  The town of Kiryat Arba symbolizes the Jewish return to its ancient lands, and Nir College is the heart of Kiryat Arba. From the ranks of our graduates come the young leaders of new settlements, as well as outstanding Torah educations.

Gary Cooperburg, the director of public relations for Kiryat Arba and once a spokesman for Meir Kahane's Kach Party, was standing in front of me. He spoke quietly, but firmly, with a heavy New York accent. He believes that 'Arabs' (we had an ongoing battle; he smirked slightly every time I said Palestinian and would quickly say Arab a trifle louder) have the right to live and work in the land of Israel but not to participate in the government. 'This is my state and it belongs to the Jewish people.'
  'But you're from New York.'
  Gary Cooperburg smiled. He was not flustered. 'A Jew is one who is born of a Jewish mother, or converts according to the law of Judaism.'
  'So, if I convert according to the law, I have more right to live here than a Palestinian farmer whose ancestors have lived on this land for the last thousand years?'

Gary Cooperburg was an expert on biblical history and he pointed out several things. First, there is no such thing as a Palestinian. He does not acknowledge them 'as a people'. They are Arabs and part of tribes, probably originating in Saudi Arabia or Egypt, and they are squatting on his land. Secondly, Jews have always lived in Judaea and Samaria (biblical Hebrew kingdoms in what is now the West Bank) and have the historic right to settle there. Thirdly, every morning when he goes to pray at the Cave of Machpelah, the burial place of the patriarchs, Cooperburg has to fear for his life because of the intifada. Is this right? That morning, for example, the last day of Ramadan, he was told he could not pray, by the Jewish army no less. 'Because the Muslims were praying. And I was reduced to praying outside the wall. Is this right?' All this, he said bitterly, is the fault of the Jewish government, who are far too easy on the Palestinians.

We continued our conversation after his lecture. Hebron is an Arab town, considered the most Islamic in the West Bank, with a population of sixty thousand Palestinian residents. Is the Jewish presence not slightly inflammatory?

Gary Cooperburg thought for a minute. Rather than complain about the Palestinians (Arabs), he decided to air his grievances about the IDF, saying that they are not nearly hard enough on the Arabs and 'every month I have to teach a whole new group of soldiers what my rights are, because they are reservists who change every month. For instance, we take our lives into our hands when we drive to Jerusalem.'

In some ways I can understand Gary Cooperburg's fears. He is the father of two. He lives behind barbed wire and drives everywhere behind plastic windows, subsidized by the government. What I cannot understand is why he stays and why he does not go back to the South Bronx, where he taught in high school before he had a religious conversion.

'I used to go to the synagogue only once in a while, and then I began studying and reading and I started to question why so many innocent people perished in the Holocaust just because they were Jews.'

He decided to make aliya – settle in Israel – in 1980, and nearly ruined his marriage by bringing his wife first to a settlement in Gaza, later to Kiryat Arba. Now she is completely adjusted, except for the plastic windows and the barbed wire. 'One adapts,' he said cynically.

And things are only getting worse. In 1987 Cooperburg's car was burnt 'because I was a Jew. Because they said they want my country! I don't call that an uprising, I call it a revolution. My reaction is to get out and kill my attackers. The very fact that my government licenses individuals to carry guns means that we have to protect ourselves.

'They want this country! They want the whole thing, not a two-state solution. It's a strategy to destroy my country.' He had a solution, he said. Did I want to hear it?

I was afraid to, but I nodded, giving him encouragement.

He grew very excited. 'Step one, repeal all citizenship of all non-Jews. Step two, make it illegal to advocate the concept of Palestinian people and state. Any Arab who wants to stand by that can stay, any others have to leave.' He checked my reaction, and I asked him to go on. Step three was slightly obscure. He said that at this stage he was sure that 'the hard core terrorists would surface. We would have to act appropriately. No more tear-gas, no more bullets. We've created this monster.' I was not sure what he was advocating. A nuclear bomb? It reeked faintly of survivalism.

'No one can tell me that a nation that won a war in six days against seven Arab countries cannot contain a revolution of women and children. They live freely and I'm afraid to walk around! That's not normal!'

We reverted to history. Gary Cooperburg said that throughout history Jews had always wanted to be good Jews, even in Germany. 'We never threw rocks. We were convicted of stealing bread to feed babies.' Exactly what this meant was unclear, but he continued. In 1948, he said, after the War of Independence when Palestine was partitioned, the Arabs should have been expelled 'because that is what nations do. We should eliminate them, not in the Mafia sense, but deport them. I don't recognize the legitimacy of the Palestinian. If they want to do it from afar, fine. But not in my country.'

The case was closed. We made some small talk about the future. Gary Cooperburg had a strong desire that Israel would become religious. 'I hope that eventually it will become a religious state. It will happen. This is destiny. Jewish destiny.'

He gave me some literature to read, pointed the way out, smiled warmly and wished me good-day.

One Sunday I drove to Ariel, six hundred metres above sea level, deep in the Ephraim hills, the fastest expanding 'town' in the West Bank. It was a few days before Ariel's bar mitzvah, its thirteenth birthday. The town was swamped with tanned couples in Ray-Bans and surfing shorts looking at skeletons of houses and building sites. In the background workmen prepared the bar mitzvah, setting up the fireworks and getting ready for the televised rock concerts. 'We are the biggest town in Samaria, the second largest in the country,' I was told by Dina Shalit, the happy public relations manager of Ariel. She is an American, her husband is an American, but her children are *sabras*, born in Israel. They are all settlers.

Ariel was founded in 1978 when two tents were dropped by a helicopter on to the stony hillside, and it is now yuppy land. The people here do not believe in Jewish destiny or a religious state.

They believe in cheap housing and the shortest possible commuting time to Tel Aviv. They have created the enormous housing boom in Ariel, lured by the government's heavy subsidies: three-bedroomed apartments for forty-two thousand pounds, a villa for eighty-three thousand pounds. Much cheaper than Tel Aviv. There are currently ten thousand residents in Ariel, almost twice as many as there were in December 1987. Dina told me that twelve hundred new housing units had already been bought and three thousand were to be built in 1992. 'Mortgages are easier to get here,' she said with a smile.

Fear is not so much a factor at Ariel as it is at Kiryat Arba. The intifada exists, it is right outside the door, but somehow it is not as threatening as it is in Hebron. And there are 'positive' changes: for instance, Dina told me, the trans-Samaria road, linking Ariel with neighbouring Jewish settlements and the Tel Aviv area, was being widened from two to four lanes to accommodate the growing population. You drive with plastic windows, but you can somehow blot out the intifada outside.

Dina gave me the demographic figures for Ariel. 'It's a young place, essentially not religious. Eighty per cent are secular Jews, twenty per cent are religious; fifty per cent Ashkenazi, fifty per cent Sephardi. It's typical of a young, upwardly mobile community.' Sixty per cent commute to Tel Aviv, thirty per cent work in local industry. The rest work in the municipality and run the shops.

These are not pioneers like Ed, these are thirtysomethings. I watched a beautiful pregnant Israeli woman, wearing Day-Glo leggings and cat sunglasses, argue with her husband in the frame of a house. 'Why didn't you tell me they were wooden houses?' she screeched. 'I am not living in a wooden house. No protection. I am not going to live in a house unless it is made of stone. Remember the war?' She stormed off.

In the middle of Ariel is an enormous communal swimming pool; around it lounged the latest imports, Soviet Jews. In 1991 more than 150,000 Soviet immigrants arrived in Israel and 1,500 of them are living in Ariel. 'This is good, good air. I meet good people, younger people,' said the elderly Jenia Mitnakoff, formerly from Leningrad, where, she said, she had been the victim of anti-Semitic 'organizations'.

'Tell them about the swastikas on your door,' prompted Dina.

'Ah yes, the swastikas on my door,' echoed Jenia.

'And what about the intifada?' I said. 'Do you feel the intifada here? Do you find it difficult to live in the middle of the trouble?'

'What trouble?' Jenia shrugged. 'Not important. When I was in Leningrad, I was part of the blockade during the Second World War. That was trouble. If I lived through that, I can live through anything.'

'But what about the Palestinians? Do you think they should be allowed to live in the West –'

'Let's go,' Dina interrupted. Jenia lifted her hand and waved goodbye. When I looked back, she was spreading suntan lotion on her shoulders.

Further along the pool were two Soviet women from Kharkov, near the Ukraine, both in red bikinis with enormous white bellies. They had been engineers at the scientific institute there, and were now working in a factory.

'It is not so bad, but the work is awful,' complained Lena, flashing a gold tooth.

'But she is delighted to be in Israel, aren't you?' prompted Dina. 'She is delighted to be living in a free country!'

Lena smiled and gazed towards the pool, but did not look so sure. 'Now there are nine of us in a house here, in Leningrad there were four.' Dina led me away. 'The thing about the Soviets,' she said later, 'is they complain a lot. The Ethiopian Jews are different. They're happy with everything you give them.' But the Ethopian Jews, who were airlifted into Israel in May 1991, are not to be seen at Ariel. Most of them are in 'absorption' centres in Galilee, learning how to use the lavatory and speak Hebrew.

Ariel had just opened its first hotel, with another pool and an artificial waterfall. I doubted that anyone would come to this desolate place. But I was wrong. On Rosh Hashanah weekend all the rooms were filled, mostly with guests from the coastal plain. 'We expect three things to bring even more people here,' Dina said. 'The college, our industry and tourism. Israelis like to go away. We want to encourage them to come here for the weekend.'

We drove up to the ridge of the hillside, past the College of Judaea and Samaria that is part of Ariel, for a view of the entire settlement. Twelve kilometres of red roofs. There was the soccer field, the central bus station, the factory that makes electronics and laser equipment and the factory that makes textiles and plastics. We talked quietly about James Baker's forthcoming eighth visit to the Middle East and the peace talks. I asked how she felt about America turning on the economic pressure and if the settlers would ever compromise. She laughed cynically. 'There are nearly a quarter of a million Jews in Judaea and Samaria. If anyone thinks this will be like the Sinai retreat, they are making a big, big mistake,' she said, referring to the settler land that was given back to Egypt in 1982. 'There is no compromise,' she added.

In the distance was an Arab village. I could see the flat roofs if I looked hard enough, the scattered tops of the olive trees. 'Before the intifada,' Dina said, 'we could have breakfast in the Arab village. Now, I would never do that. That does make me sad.'

We stood quietly, looking out towards the town. Dina

mentioned that Ariel had started off as a dream, and now it was a reality. 'You can make your dreams come true. Amazing, isn't it?' she said proudly. 'By 1995 we will triple our population.'

5. A Generation of Hate

The old children's taunt goes, 'Sticks and stones may break my bones, but words can never hurt me.' It applies to Israel the other way around. It is the words and pictures of young Palestinians defying the Israeli army after 20 years of occupation, with no end in sight, that are bringing the region a new sense of urgent crisis.

Flora Lewis, *The New York Times*, 1988

The Arabs all say they identify with the cause, so let them suffer for it.

Guela Cohen (Member of the Israeli Knesset)

Since I am drowning, why should I fear getting wet?

Palestinian proverb

Mary Khass, an early educator in the Gaza Strip, can always tell what has happened in the refugee camps by the behaviour of the children the next morning. If someone has been shot, the children will pair off and play games like soldiers and resisters or Palestinians and Jews; if a parent has been taken to prison, they will put black plastic bags over their tiny heads and pretend they are the torturers. The smallest ones, five and six years old, are often the most imaginative: they turn over their desks and pretend they are Israeli jeeps; their building blocks become guns; dolls fight in hand-to-hand combat. The tragedies that their parents live with every day – arrests, killings, funerals, demonstrations – are acted out in the children's play. Throughout it all Mary Khass, who is sixty-four and grew up in Haifa during the British occupation of Palestine, stands behind the children, watching, worrying, but not intervening.

'I never try to stop them,' Khass says. 'I try to teach the little ones that the intifada is a revolution of life, not of death. But they don't seem to understand that. When all children can see is a dark, dark future, martyrdom becomes a glorious achievement. Before the intifada I used to tell my friends we have to beware of a generation that sees nothing but occupied and occupier. Now what you see is far worse. It's not an example of the intifada, but an extreme reaction to desperation. They think, what the hell? What could happen that's worse than the way that I'm living?'

Sometimes when she is particularly tired, or she feels especially sensitive to the tension in the camps that day, she thinks about her own childhood during the last days of the British mandate. She remembers the British soldiers in the streets, drunk on a Saturday night. She remembers the difficulties of everyday life in Haifa during the late 1940s. She remembers the curfews and the barbed wire when she was a child of eight or nine, a student in an Anglican school. She hated that school, hated the reminder that the country was occupied by the British; she hated singing 'God Save the King' and being grateful to the God-fearing British ladies who visited the students. 'I shirked them. I hated the Lady Bountiful attitude of the British. I rebelled, and my education was about the heroes and the partisans. I became who I am through that. A fighter, an activist, a peace advocate, a feminist.'

There is one incident she always remembers. It was December, it was freezing cold, and she was standing in a long queue at the post office, waiting to buy stamps. Ahead of her was a Palestinian boy of her own age. She watched as he was approached by a British soldier who took out his gun and offered to sell it to the Palestinian. The boy handed the soldier three Palestinian pounds. The soldier took the money and looked the other way as the boy hid the gun in the folds of his jacket.

They waited in the cold to buy stamps, Mary blowing on her hands to keep them warm, the boy shuffling his feet. When they were at the head of the queue, the same soldier was near the top searching other Palestinians for weapons. When he saw the boy, he smiled. Then he searched him, found the gun and began to beat him. He laughed as he took back the gun from the boy who had just paid him three pounds for it. He moved down the queue and sold it to another Palestinian who bought it for three pounds. 'When I think of frustration,' Khass said, 'I think of that.'

During the Gulf War Khass had a special permit from the Israeli Civil and Military Administration Office to go out during curfew. Because she was one of the few people who were allowed out, she delivered pay cheques to some of her employees who were at home and needed money. She had to collect the cheques, then go to each house in each refugee camp, get a signature, take the cheques to the bank, cash them and return them to the camps; one day it took her thirteen hours to deliver ninety-three cheques.

Sometimes, in the camps, she would stay in the enclosed houses long enough to see the children, and observe the effect the twenty-four-hour curfew had on their behaviour. 'But it's not easy for an outsider to understand what it's like to be in a camp under curfew if you are a child. Inside your house with maybe fourteen other people all day long, and then you go to sleep. The schools are always closed. There is nothing to play with but sewage.

'What do you expect, what kind of behaviour do you think you will see, from children who constantly see their parents humiliated? Who see terror? Who are frightened? Their fear and reality is something that they can't cope with.'

One afternoon she was driving out of Beach camp, one of the most populated refugee camps, on her way to deliver a cheque when a soldier stopped her and asked for her special permit. She gave it to him. Perhaps there was something in her manner, a touch of what he perceived as arrogance or flippancy, that annoyed him. 'Arab whore!' he spat at her, and handed back the permit. When she protested, he looked at her and said, 'Shut up before I kill you.'

Khass said nothing. She took the permit from the soldier, put it in her wallet and drove on to deliver the next cheque. But as she drove, she remembered something else. Once, walking through a Jewish area in Jerusalem, the Jewish woman in front of her spotted an old Arab man across the street. The woman froze and called out to her neighbours in horror, 'Aravim! Aravim!' For a moment Mary, walking quietly behind the woman, also froze. Her first thought was, please, God, don't let them find out I'm an Arab. Her second was outrage. 'I felt so ashamed of my reaction. It's the same when I'm travelling, watching people's expressions change the moment they read my travel document and see that I am Palestinian. The fear on their faces . . . It's not easy to live without an identity, to be treated on a subhuman level because of your nationality.'

The night after delivering the cheques Khass was listening to the radio at home with her husband. The news included a feature about the yellow stars that the Jews were forced to wear under Nazi occupation, and Mary Khass became hysterical. She began to laugh at what she perceived as the terrible irony of it all and suddenly she was laughing so hard that she could not breathe, and her husband was watching her with concern.

Later she grew pensive. 'During the Gulf War we were worse than trash. Our lives were in danger. One of my neighbours was in labour, and when her husband went outside to get the car to bring her to the hospital, the soldiers beat him up.' She thought about how a Jew would feel walking with a yellow star in occupied Poland, or France, the humiliation, and then she visualized herself that day in the street in Jerusalem when the Jewish woman called out in horror, 'Aravim! Aravim!'

Khass let the children in her school play soldiers and resisters and Palestinians and Jews because it was 'one way of them coping and understanding. But it shows us having to cope with a coming generation of angry, vicious people. What bothers me most is that in the refugee camps the children know no other reality. Anger turns into viciousness. Confusion into viciousness. They become reckless. Children of ten throwing stones, challenging their destiny.'

From the start of the intifada in December 1987 until June 1992 1,075 Palestinians have been killed, though the figures are extremely difficult to calculate. The Palestinian sources give a number that seems inflated, the Israelis a much lower one. The army says that the Palestinians count every heart attack in their figures, and the Palestinians naturally deny this.

According to a report prepared by the Jerusalem Media Communication Committee, approximately 450 of the 1,075 dead were children under the age of eighteen, who play a more active role in the intifada than anyone. Seventy-nine of the children killed in the past four years have been under twelve, and 343 were between the ages of thirteen and eighteen. The majority of the deaths are from gunshots; the other main killer is tear-gas.

The judicial system under occupation is stringent. Reports prepared by human rights groups say that as many as half of the

Palestinians arrested and held in detention – for throwing stones and for other acts of defiance – have been under the age of eighteen. Since the beginning of the intifada the legal criminal age has been reduced from sixteen to fourteen and then to twelve. Israeli judges have been advised to take great care when examining those under fourteen. On 20 January 1988 the *Jerusalem Post* quoted some figures:

The Israeli opposition estimates that over 25 per cent of the more than 50,000 Palestinians in Israeli jails now are minors. 'They are just taken off the streets, even when there is no sign of trouble,' one Israeli human rights demonstrator said. 'Their parents do not know where they are being held. We hear so many stories, beatings, overcrowded cells.' Knesset member Dedi Zucker, asked to comment on the 25 per cent estimate, said, 'More than a thousand minors? That seems a reasonable estimate.'

Children become involved in the intifada the moment they are old enough to throw a stone or walk to a street demonstration. In his article 'A Profile of the Stone Throwers' in the *Journal of Palestine Studies* (spring 1988) the writer Daoud Kuttab described the part that young children are expected to play in the intifada. According to Kuttab, teachers and other intifada leaders, including their parents, assign tasks to the children:

Age 7–10: set tyres on fire in the middle of the road to block traffic.

Age 11–14: place large stones in the middle of the road, use slings and slingshots.

Age 15–17: throw large rocks, activities aimed at bypassing curfew.

Human rights groups, including Amnesty International, claim the Israeli army's response to the intifada is to increase their oppressive measures. Shooting and killing, detention without trial, curfew, breaking bones and using tear-gas are the most commonly used methods. Because they see the Palestinian schools and universities as 'breeding grounds' for the rebellion, they were closed by military orders (though all have since reopened). The overall effect of the intifada on the lives of the Palestinian children has been devastating, not only from the psychological viewpoint but also because of the loss of school days.

The most frightening thing about the children is their nonchalance. They were all born under occupation, as refugees, and know no other way of life. These are children who throw stones at soldiers with absolutely no fear, who have learned words like Molotov and martyr and war by the age of five and who look at me with a mixture of horror or amusement when I ask them if they know any Jewish children. They are not afraid to die. Some of these children have become so resilient that they do not blink an eye when they see their fathers dragged off in the middle of the night by soldiers; others are petrified by the sound of the soldiers' jeeps or gunshots. Mary Khass calls these children, in a tired voice, the next generation.

The Israeli response is varied. 'We are not monsters. We do not want to shoot children,' one soldier in Gaza told me. 'But these are not children. When they are coming at you with a stone in their hand and they are screaming "Allahu Akbah", you feel terrified. When you are on patrol, you are vulnerable, maybe just as vulnerable as they are.' Riding in the back of an exposed army jeep, you can see the kind of panic, the tenseness the soldiers must feel.

Another reserve captain, who was in his early forties, said 'I served in the Yom Kippur War and that was not nearly as bad as being on reserve duty in Nablus. There the Palestinian kids were throwing rocks from rooftops in the Old City and we could not see them coming. I was there a week after Israeli soldiers were killed in the Old City by rocks thrown on their heads, and it was not easy.'

The Israelis back up their argument: they see the children as extremists who are being used by the PLO. In a report called 'Children as Participants in the Intifada', which was prepared by the Israeli Ministry of Justice 'in response to persistent criticism from various human rights groups of Israeli policy on children', the government position is clear:

Children of all ages are recruited by the PLO and extremist Islamic elements to participate in the street violence: they roll tyres into the road and set them aflame; they make roadblocks out of boulders and they throw stones and other dangerous objects at Israeli civilians and soldiers . . .

International law forbids the use of civilians as shields in order to impede military operations (see, e.g., Article 28 of the Fourth Geneva Convention of 1949). Jean Pictet, in the Official Red Cross Commentary on Article 28, notes that the use of civilians as shields has been condemned as cruel and barbaric. By analogy, terrorist groups which place their operational headquarters in civilian areas, as the PLO has done in Lebanon, have been criticized. Furthermore, Article 38 of the unanimously adopted United Nations Convention on the Rights of the Child (1989) condemns the recruitment and involvement of children under 15 years old in hostilities and armed conflicts. Since the outset, the intifada has exploited children by placing them in harm's way. Thus it is the inciters, and not the IDF, who must ultimately be held responsible for the injury and death of rioting children.

But not all the children who were shot were throwing stones. According to Swedish Save the Children, 'nearly one-quarter of the 159 child deaths reported in the first two years of the intifada were a result of tear-gas exposure. Thousands of other children required medical treatment after exposure to gas. Yet Israeli officials have consistently denied, without investigation, that child deaths and many serious injuries have resulted from inhalation of tear-gas.'

There are also the reports of journalists. 'The result of Rabin's strategy of "force, power and blows" can be seen in the crowded casualty ward of the Shifa Hospital, Gaza's biggest medical centre,' Eric Silver wrote in the *Observer* at the beginning of the intifada.

An Arab doctor said that the centre had treated 200 people since the beginning of the week, most of them suffering from broken elbows and knees. Three had fractured skulls. The doctor, who declined to give his name because the Israelis had barred hospital staff from speaking to the press, said most of the casualties were boys and young men between 13 and 30. About 25 were older men and women. Three pregnant women had suffered and their homes were tear-gassed.

At the beginning of the intifada another practice that was popular with soldiers was breaking the hands of the stone throwers, sometimes finger by finger, as if to teach them a lesson they would never forget. *Ha'aretz*, the Israeli daily newspaper, claimed in January 1988 that the Israel Defence Ministry had ordered ten thousand batons of 'finest quality' hardwood, apparently for issue to troops in the West Bank and Gaza. The *Jerusalem Post* wrote:

Some soldiers still don't have riot control equipment and are presumably expected to kick Palestinians and hit them with bare fists and rifle butts. This method is considered more effective than detention. A detainee sent to Fara's prison will be freed within 18 days unless the authorities have enough evidence to charge him. He may then resume throwing stones at soldiers. But if the troops break his hand, he won't be able to throw stones for a month and a half.

But that tactic rarely worked. As soon as a child was released from hospital, he would be back on the streets, if not throwing stones, passing out leaflets or torching tyres.

'We are not concerned with suffering, we are concerned with building an independent Palestinian state. We don't consider living under occupation living like human beings,' said Mustafa El-Hamadid Min, the father of a 21-year-old boy who had been shot in the head by soldiers two weeks before I interviewed him in the spring of 1989 in a small village near Silwan. He spoke quickly, pausing occasionally to stare down at his hands folded neatly in his lap. His two other sons were in jail – one in Ansar 3 – and he claimed that just the day before his teenage daughter had been beaten up and dragged into the village well by soldiers. 'She screamed and she screamed, and her mother ran out to try to beat them off, but what could she do? The soldiers were laughing. To them, it is funny.'

Despite the recent death in the family, the atmosphere that day in the two-roomed mud-floored house, home to fifteen people, was alive, almost cheerful.

Mustafa's wife and sister and three of the children sat in one corner making sweets for Ramadan, and the youngest of Mustafa's sixteen children, a nine-month-old baby, crawled on the bed in the centre of the room. His twelve-year-old son Ahmed poured tea into glasses and served biscuits from a tin. Mustafa showed me a video of his son in the Palestinian equivalent of a Boy Scout uniform, receiving an award a few weeks before he died. 'He liked to go camping,' his father said. There were no tears. He watched the video intently but dry eyed; to have a martyr for a son is an enormous honour.

Mustafa is a survivor. He was eight years old on 9 April 1948 when a group of Jewish guerrillas composed of the Irgun and the Stern Gang invaded his village during the War of Independence and wiped out 250 people, in what later became known as the Deir Yassin massacre. He and his sister hid in a cave for two days and when they emerged, they picked over the littered bodies until they found their family, most of them dead. They began walking out of the village, not knowing where they would go. When he thought of his past, Mustafa said that he saw a long dark tunnel, and it was all sadness.

'All that we have ever known is the occupation,' he said. 'And for us, the intifada is food, is nourishment to the Palestinian people.' He turned back to the video and talked about his son's death. 'I heard the shots and then one of the villagers told me that it was my son who was martyred,' he said. 'I passed out. When I woke up, I was at the hospital. They never let me see his body. At the cemetery when he was buried, the soldiers tear-gassed our village. Ten people were wounded.'

I asked him why the Israelis tear-gassed the village. They would not fire tear-gas unless they were provoked, I prodded. 'There was a demonstration,' he said glumly.

'Was your son throwing stones at soldiers when they shot him? Was he politically active?'

The younger son said, 'Of course he was. Everyone is.'

Mustafa dropped his head and stirred four teaspoons of sugar into his tea. 'The intifada has been twenty-two years in the making. We will not be held down any longer. And we know that by the death of our children freedom is coming.'

The children are imperative to the movement. When Palestinian children dream at night, they say they dream about soldiers and guns, helicopters and killing Jews. Once I sat in a pre-school in Hizma, a little village near Jerusalem that is quiet and remote. The pre-school is an alternative kindergarten, set up by Asya Habash, who heads the Early Childhood Resource Centre in East Jerusalem. The centre attempts to train local women as teachers with a 'humanistic, developmental approach', even though all they have is a room without running water and without outdoor facilities.

'Often we train teachers to make materials for the children out of scraps; matchboxes, juice cans, you name it, we use it,' said Habash. 'We are unable to reach the children all the time, because of curfews and strikes, and our biggest obstacle is keeping the schools open, to sustain them, to give the children a normal existence, to get them away from the stress of home.' Habash and her group also produced a booklet for mothers on how to cope with children and the intifada, addressing issues like bedwetting, anxiety, sleep disorders.

Hizma looks like one of the faded black and white photographs of the West Bank taken in the 1920s: gentle, rolling hills, clean white houses and women in long embroidered Palestinian dresses balancing baskets of produce on their heads. 'This school has one of the most emotionally stable groups of children because Hizma is a quiet village,' said Sulaima Abu-Haja, a teacher who had been trained in the Piaget technique while living in California. But beyond the hills Hizma is surrounded by the skeletons of Jewish settlements that are quickly springing up on what the Palestinian children think of as their land, and they are aware of the tension that encloses them. All of them, according to Sulaima, have in some way been affected. 'At the beginning of the intifada the look on their faces was painful. Now it's matter of fact. It's small talk. And that is what scares me.'

I sat on the floor of the Hizma school with the children, three- to five-year-olds, and watched them draw pictures with coloured pens of prisons ('this is where my father is'), strange aeroplanes ('Iraqi jets to save us') and big men with sticks ('soldiers who hit my brother'). When I asked them if they knew any Jewish children with whom they could play, they looked at me with wide, startled eyes.

'Yahoud?'

'No, they don't know any Jewish children,' answered Sulaima in an amused voice. At lunchtime they went outside and played on the slide and the swings and sang Ramadan, as opposed to intifada, songs. A local woman came to bring the teachers sweet bread and tea, which she carried on a tray on her head, and there was such a feeling of peace that I could forget – if I did not look in the distance and see the settlements.

'It's like Sleepy Hollow, this place,' said one of the teachers' helpers. But there have been incidents: several houses have been demolished, and more recently a youth stabbed a soldier and then took refuge in the village. Hizma was put under curfew and helicopters flew overhead. They did not find the boy for one month. He was fourteen.

Madeha was five, very pretty and intensely shy. She stood apart from the other children when they played. Her father had been sentenced to sixteen years in prison, of which he had already served four. She had seen him a handful of times, but there were constant reminders: the photographs in the house, the visits to prison, the intifada songs. Her mother told her that her father was a hero.

'Where is your father?' I said, kneeling next to her on the ground.

She looked at me and carefully curled and uncurled a piece of tissue until it was in shreds. She hid it behind her hair and shrugged. 'In prison. Because he had a green identity card and they caught him.'

'Is your mother sad?'

She turned away and picked up a crayon and began to scratch at a piece of paper. 'No.'

She started to draw: 'My country.' Angry slashes of red, green, black, the Palestinian flag. A blue house with a television antenna: 'House for Jewish settlers. An army jeep and police and Iraqi helicopters. And a man.'

'What is the man called?'

'Wasef. My father.'

Muhammed was six and more outgoing. He watched the house next door being demolished. 'The army started shooting at the wall. And the woman started shouting. The wife of the man who owned the house started screaming. The army brought a bulldozer and began to knock down the walls. We stood on our balcony and watched.'

'Muhammed, what is the intifada?'

He looked at me quietly. 'I'll tell you tomorrow. No, I'll tell you now.' He narrowed his eyes. 'The intifada is like Tom and Jerry. The dog follows the cat and then he eats the cat. Another cat comes and bites the dog and he eats that cat too. That's what the intifada is.'

'Who is the cat?' I bent down and sat next to him.

He did not answer immediately but continued to draw: a policeman clubbing a man. 'The intifada is a demonstration and people hold flags. They're demonstrating because the Jews hold flags and the Jews are demolishing our country.'

'Do you know any Jews?'

Muhammed said no, but he could draw them. He drew a soldier with a gun and a walkie-talkie, which he named in Hebrew, *makhshir kesher*. 'Some settlers came to my aunt's house and started shooting and the Jewish children were on their bikes. They shot because we put flags on the electric wires.'

He explained to me in detail how to hang a Palestinian flag from the live wire. 'First, tie a stone, like this, round the flag. Then you swing and throw it on the wire until it stays. Sometimes they burn down, or the army makes us climb up and take them down, but if not, you have Palestine.'

Muhammed drew another picture. He entitled it 'The Palestinian Flag and the Jews'. An empty prison, a flag and a soldier ('a Jew') capturing a boy 'because he threw stones'. More jeeps, more Scuds. He drew a more chilling picture, maybe to impress me, of a Palestinian man stabbing a Jew. It startled me. I sat down with him, a tiny child with a round face jabbing at his paper with his coloured pen.

'But look, there is hope,' pointed out Sulaima, who stood watching and could understand the sadness that I felt. 'He drew the sun shining in the distance.'

I moved from the towns to see the children in the camps. They climbed an electric wire to raise a handmade Palestinian flag, knowing very well that one of their friends had been electrocuted the week before. They would throw a stone at a soldier at a demonstration because a communiqué issued by the Unified Leadership for the Uprising had told them to, well aware that if they were caught, they would be beaten. Education comes second: what is important is to learn how to burn a tyre and how to make a Molotov cocktail.

'They were born under the occupation and they know no other way of life,' said Felicia Langer. 'And because dying represents the ultimate act of heroism and patriotism, they grow up without fear.'

'They are different, because if they hear gunshots outside the door, they have learned how to cope with it,' said Dr Cairo Arafat, who had been studying the effect of the intifada on Palestinian children. 'They don't panic. They are calm and orderly. They get up and lock the door and shut the windows.'

One stiflingly hot night in April 1989 I sat on the floor of a small house in a closed village near Jerusalem, after curfew. I had come to see Amal Labadi, a woman whose husband and brother-in-law were about to be deported, and who was active in the feminist arm of the DFLP faction of the PLO. The Labadi family at that time were watched by the authorities. The women were under house arrest, every move they made was monitored. Still they took enormous chances, publishing illegal newsletters, meeting with wanted men, distributing literature. They worked defiantly, with a kind of steadfast, detached patience that I found slightly chilling.

Amal's husband, Muhammed (*nom de guerre* Abu Samer), and his younger brother, Majid, were both well known as activists in the DFLP. In their book *Intifada* the Israeli reporters Ze'ev Schiff and Ehud Ya'ari claim that it was Muhammed Labadi who was responsible for taking the intifada from Gaza to Jerusalem in December 1987:

Since Jerusalem was still virgin territory, Muhammed Labadi decided to go ahead for two aims with one effort: to set the city alight, thus bringing the violence to Israel's doorstep: and to do so by a deliberate, controlled effort of PLO activists. His scheme was to bring in volunteers from Gaza and Hebron as the agents for importing the riots to Jerusalem. Emissaries were dispatched to mobilize these youngsters.

But eighteen months later Muhammed and Majid were both in prison awaiting deportation orders, and their house had become a house of women. Their children grow up in the shadow of absent fathers, and their mothers talk of things that they cannot understand: 'resisting the occupation', 'demonstration', 'uprising'. Jordanian television was blasting in the small house and there were grainy, black and white photographs of the brothers on the wall. With me were a German woman psychiatrist, who was travelling through the Middle East documenting torture and its effect on families, and a photographer, Marc Schlossman; she was sitting at a table scribbling notes while he was on the floor beside four small children, who were waving photographs of their soon-to-be missing father and singing an intifada song.

Amal Labadi watched the children as army jeeps raced up and down the street outside. 'None of us have fear, even the children,' she said, showing the smallest child how to hold his two fingers up in a victory sign. 'They are working for freedom as much as the grown-ups.'

She motioned for them to line up and sing for me. The children laughed and obeyed:

> 'We went down to the streets,
> we hold the flags,
> we give thanks for our homeland
> with the most beautiful songs.
> Songs for national unity,
> songs for popular war and revolution
> show the way for independence.
> All my homeland be glad.
> There are children who arouse,
> who understand our cause,
> and, holding stones in their hands,
> they are challenging the occupation.
> They are burning the tyres and stones.
> But the sun will come out from this
> and there will be thousands and thousands of daylights.'

'Where is your father?' Marc asked one child.

'In prison,' the boy, aged about three, answered blithely.

'When do you see him?'

'On days when I go to prison to see my husband he screams and screams,' interrupted his mother.

There was something highly disturbing about a house empty of men and full of women, about children singing intifada songs before they were old enough to know the meaning. The German psychiatrist talked about Palestinian family unities. 'They have a kind of core, a closeness that most families in normal circumstances do not have.'

We stayed for a few hours talking to the children and to Amal. When we left, we backed out in our tinny Palestinian rented car – blue plates – and swerved into the dirt road leading east, towards Jerusalem. Ahead was a roadblock; soldiers were swarming all over the village, looking for someone.

At the roadblock we were stopped. A spotlight was shone into the car and a soldier stuck an Uzi in the driver's open window. The German psychiatrist, Barbara, blanched. She muttered something in German. Suddenly I knew what was worrying her. I had forgotten the package of leaflets that Amal Labadi had asked us to take back to Jerusalem for her; it was stowed neatly in the back seat, tied with a cord. I had felt uneasy about it but had thought, what the hell, what could possibly be in it? Not wanting to disappoint Amal, who had been generous with her time, and not wanting to feel guilty, Barbara and I had looked at each other and agreed to take it.

'What are you doing here?' said the soldier with the Uzi, aged maybe eighteen, with round glasses and a small growth of beard.

From the back seat Barbara said, 'Visiting friends.'

He jumped back. 'Friends! In an Arab village?'

Silence.

'You cannot have Arabs for friends. What are their names?' He pointed at me in the passenger seat. 'What are the names of your friends?'

I shrugged and replied, 'I don't remember.'

'You don't remember their names!' he said in an incredulous voice.

Behind him another soldier spoke rapidly in Hebrew.

'Give us your passports, please.'

One German and two American passports were produced. The soldier was more confused.

'I don't understand. How can you have Arabs as friends? You are Americans. You' – he turned to Marc, whose father is Jewish and who has a Jewish surname, but who was not raised as a Jew – 'are a Jew?'

Marc cleared his throat and said, 'My father is Jewish . . .' He drifted off. He finds it disorientating in Israel when Israelis look at him, baffled, and say, 'Are you a Jew?'

'Either you're a Jew or you're not a Jew!' the soldier shouted.

I said to Marc, 'Just tell him you're Jewish. Does it really matter?'

Marc did as I suggested. Barbara shifted uncomfortably in the back seat. The soldier, clearly nonplussed, fingered the passports.

'I don't understand. You are a Jew and you are with Arabs?' He looked through the stamps. 'Why were you in Turkey, in Nicaragua? What is the nature of your work in Israel?'

He kept us for ten minutes, radioing in to headquarters with the passport. Marc idly played with the radio dial. Barbara covered the leaflets with her jacket.

'Which hotel do you stay at in Jerusalem? Where did you meet the Arabs?'

Barbara named the hostel in Jerusalem where she was staying.

'No, we don't remember their names. Yes, we met them in Jerusalem. No, I don't remember how we met them.'

The soldier was either feeling generous or bored.

'OK, go, and don't come back. This is a closed military area.'

I thought of asking to see his military papers, knowing he did not have any, but I was too relieved to see the back of the spotlight, the back of his Uzi. When we got to Jerusalem, Barbara and I dumped the leaflets that Amal had given us in the nearest bin.

*

At school in Gaza Mary Khass tries to take the children aside, to play with them alone, to give them privacy and space and to allow them to act out their aggression. Sometimes their reactions astound her; at other times she feels overwhelmed by futility and helplessness. She remembers the incident that showed her she was teaching children who had completely lost their innocence. One of the brightest students, five-year-old Muhammed, refused to speak for one week. At the end of the week, alarmed by his silence, Khass held his hand and managed to prise the story out of him. She found out something had happened to him.

Night-time in the refugee camp is when soldiers roam the camps and raid houses at random, and the mulathameen carry out their activities. Collaborators are often killed after dark and people are taken away for interrogation. Families huddle in their houses, unable to leave, to visit neighbours, to walk down the street. The silence that settles over Gaza after 8.00 p.m. is like a shroud. (The curfew in Gaza usually lasts from 8.00 p.m. to 4.00 a.m. though this can vary. Sometimes, for example in feast periods, holidays or weeks of good grace, it does not begin until 10.00 p.m.)

Muhammed was woken up by banging on the door in the middle of the night, the sound that every Palestinian dreads and knows will come eventually. This time the soldiers had selected Muhammed's father to come out and clean the streets of the refugee camp. Muhammed's father offered no resistance – what was the point? Instead he dressed quietly and left with the soldiers. Muhammed's mother held him and whispered to him to stay quiet.

His father finished the job at four in the morning, but had to wait outside in the pouring rain for the soldiers to return with his identity card, which no Palestinian can ever be without. At seven he left for work, but decided to stop first at the petrol station to have his tyre mended. Muhammed begged to be taken with him and his father agreed.

'Don't get out of the car, don't say a word if anyone comes up to you,' Muhammed's father cautioned him when he went inside to pay for the tyre.

For a few minutes Muhammed sat quietly. When he saw the Israeli army jeep pull into the station, he thought of his father standing out in the rain, and he felt the anger rise inside him. Shaking his tiny fist, he yelled out at the soldiers in Arabic. They stared at the child, bewildered. A sergeant leaped out of the jeep and grabbed him, ordering him to apologize. The five-year-old doggedly refused, so the soldiers repeated their request. Muhammed shook his head and the soldiers smacked him across the face. Then they dragged him inside to the group of Palestinian men who had witnessed the scene. Muhammed's father, exhausted after a night spent sweeping the streets, knowing that he would be taken away and lose another day of work, dropped his eyes.

'Whose brat is this?' the soldier shouted at the Palestinian men clustered near the petrol tanks.

No one answered. Muhammed looked at his father, and at that moment he realized that his father, his hero, was abandoning him.

'Whose Palestinian monster is this? Who teaches their children to be this badly behaved?'

No one answered. The soldier cuffed Muhammed on the head, warned him that next time he would take him to prison and jumped back into his jeep.

Muhammed's father came out to claim his son. 'I'm sorry. I told you to stay in the car and not to cause trouble. I just wanted to get this tyre changed and get back to work.' But Muhammed would not listen, because to him the man who had been humiliated not once but twice in front of the Israeli soldiers could not be his father. How could this man who refused to claim him be his father?

By the time Mary had extracted the story from Muhammed, he had broken bonds with his father and begun to align himself with his uncle, who lived with the family. His uncle, Muhammed said proudly, was not afraid of soldiers. He was not afraid to cause trouble, throw stones, defy authority. But his father . . . his father was afraid of the soldiers!

'How can they ever feel safe at home when home is no longer a safe place? How can they believe in their parents when they see them constantly humiliated? I tell you, this next generation, this coming generation of Palestinians, is angry, frustrated, confused and vicious, while the Israeli children are becoming increasingly arrogant because of their easy victories. And it is with these children, Israeli and Palestinian, that the future lies. Remember, children don't forget. It is always there.'

'The next generation, it's a disaster,' said one high-ranking official for the United Nations Relief and Works Agency. 'They see confrontation on the street and live with the violence: people locked up during curfews, children screaming, parents screaming. It's like a Kafkaesque world. Then there is the loss of schooling, and even if a child does go to school, he might swallow tear-gas, or he probably is not paying attention because he is thinking of other things. I am sorry,' he said, shaking his head. 'I'm a realist, not an optimist.'

Dr Ahmed Baker, a professor of psychology at Birzeit University in the West Bank, studied the impact of the intifada on a large group of children in the occupied territories. His findings are disturbing: not only will the effects of post-traumatic stress be felt on children two generations down, but 'all research indicates that the next generation of Palestinians will be radicalized as well as traumatized. Most children are not willing to make peace with Israelis, not even to accept a two-state solution,' Dr Baker said. In a similar study carried out in Lebanon four years after the 1982 Israeli invasion fifty-eight per cent of the children still experienced post-traumatic stress.

'Also, as the intifada progresses, casualty figures before the age of fifteen are rising,' Dr Baker continued. 'Younger and younger children are becoming involved.' He said this is because they are modelling themselves after older children, especially when they see the older ones reinforced positively by Palestinian society. The other reason is sheer practicality: 'the younger ones are at home, the older ones are in prison. The Israelis imprison a high number of youths.'

Among the groups of children tested Baker found that those who actively participated in the intifada had a higher level of self-esteem than those who did not: 'They feel good about themselves because they perceive themselves as agents of change. They are the vanguards of the intifada. The IDF is an army that the world respects, but these children see themselves as being able to crush that army. Although they are depressed, they think that they are going to change things.'

On one side are the angry Palestinians; on the other are the Israeli children who, Baker felt, are in danger of becoming isolated and arrogant. 'One would have to ask the question, how can Israel condone this? It's called moral disagreement. It becomes OK to kill a Palestinian if you can dehumanize the enemy. Golda Meir said there was no such thing as a Palestinian. Shamir called us grasshoppers. It starts at that level and filters down. To the Israeli children the Palestinian has become the bogeyman.' When Baker told me this, I recalled reading something in the newspapers about a child's video game that was for sale in Israel at the beginning of the intifada: it was a bit like Pac-man, only the object was to see how many Palestinians you could gun down in one go.

'The Israelis have their problems too. They have become not only vicious, but masters. They feel that they are the most intelligent, the most superior,' said Mary Khass. 'And now there are increasing problems in Israel with crime, with addiction on the rise, with young people wanting to leave the country. I'm not surprised, when they are handed a gun and taught to be soldiers when they are still teenagers.'

'Remember that we're suffering too,' said Guela Della Rosa, a fifth-generation Israeli who lost her nineteen-year-old soldier son, David, in December 1988 when his bus was fire-bombed by five Molotov cocktails. David Della Rosa, who was on his way to visit his girlfriend, managed to climb out of the bus, then realized that a young woman with two children was trapped inside. When he climbed back inside the bus, it exploded. He lingered for weeks in hospital before dying, his mother said, in agony.

Guela Della Rosa was orthodox, wore a headscarf and spoke no English. It was a few days before Passover and her flat was spotlessly clean. I sat down on a sofa covered with a lace cloth. She had another son, who was older than David and who sat next to her with his hand on her shoulder.

'She's very strong,' said the Hebrew interpreter who had brought me to Guela's flat. 'She won't cry, even when she talks about David's death.'

But after an hour of describing what she called 'this war', Guela did cry. Fingering david's Torah – which strangely enough did not burn in the fire that engulfed the bus – she said, 'There are no winners in this war. All of us, the mothers of the dead, are united in a sadness.'

At the same time Guela Della Rosa could see no immediate

solution and refused to compromise her position. 'We will never, ever, give up our land. There are other Arab countries and only one Jewish state in the world. Can't the Palestinians go to Jordan?'

Veronica Cohen describes herself as an 'orthodox liberal Jew' from West Jerusalem. Every Thursday she holds a dialogue between Jewish and Palestinian women outside Jerusalem. Often the context of the conversation is so tragic that it borders on the comical.

'One time there was a Jewish woman who could not make the next meeting because she was going dancing with her husband. One of the Palestinian women got angry and began to shout because she said that was insensitive. Her husband was in prison, so there was no way that she could ever go dancing. But at the next meeting there was a wonderful moment. One of the Jewish mothers was telling the group how worried she was because her young son, a soldier, was hitch-hiking to Gaza. She said she was so frightened for his safety she could not sleep. Then one of the Palestinian women got up and went over and hugged her and said, "I feel for you. I understand what you mean."'

Cohen smiled. 'When something like that happens, it is a triumph.'

In 1982, before the intifada, Felicia Langer wrote in her book *An Age of Stone*:

A second generation of heroes is sprouting from this land which is soaked with the blood of her children. And in the city streets there are soldiers patrolling, ready to shoot and kill instantly. The second generation of oppressors, the by-product of the occupation ... But I am convinced that, along with our second generation of oppressors, eventually a second generation of our own people will rebel against these crimes.

For the older Palestinians, there is the question of what to do with their lives. Some of them are so immersed in the intifada or in resistance that they cannot imagine a life without it, and they cannot identify with anything outside it. Amira, who was twenty-five and had lived all her life in the Jabalia camp in the Gaza Strip, talked steadily for two hours about her work in the popular committee, in the camp's women's group, in her student union. But she looked at me with amazement when I asked her about childhood.

'What do I remember of my childhood? I remember my birthday because I was born in 1967, the year the Israelis occupied our country. I remember soldiers holding guns, and playing inside barbed wire. I started my life like this, under occupation. That's how I came into this world, and that's what I remember, that's what everyone remembers. What else is there left for me to remember?'

'Sometimes I think, I am twenty-five years old and I want to live!' said Joyce, a Christian Palestinian, a beautiful woman with large, dark-blue eyes and light-brown hair that she pulled back from her face. Her father worked for a foreign airline and her English was perfect. She dressed fashionably, like an American college student. 'But it's the intifada and we're not allowed to feel that way. I feel guilty if I feel that way. But I do.'

We sat in the leafy garden of her parents' spacious house in Ramallah and ate spaghetti and drank wine. Joyce had gone to university in America, but returned at the start of the intifada because she wanted to be a part of 'history in the making'. Her husband was a professor of engineering at Birzeit University. He still lectured, but held secret classes for students at random locations. He was constantly frustrated by the restrictions. 'No computers, no supplies. Sometimes I can't believe that I pass these kids when they take exams. They're just not prepared. But still, they are learning something.'

'I can't remember the last time that I went to the cinema or to a party,' said Joyce. 'Before the intifada we went to the beach all the time. We've only gone once in the past four years, and when we got there with our picnic and we looked at each other and felt so guilty and unhappy, we packed everything and came home.'

Her wedding party was boycotted; she could not recollect when she last went to a restaurant. 'There was one opened in Ramallah a while ago, and everyone went, and then suddenly it closed,' she said. 'I think that people feel too guilty to enjoy themselves, even a little bit.'

She showed me the inside of the house attached to her parents' home where the family had stayed for the forty-three days during the Gulf War curfew. 'I have never felt so close to going crazy,' she said, walking from room to room. 'At first we played cards or read books, then you just start going mad. You pace. You pace all the time.'

Maida, who had also been educated in America and worked for the YMCA in East Jerusalem, viewed the future with a cynical eye. 'If you ask me, there is no future for us,' she said simply. 'There is only a future for the radical or the political. If you are in the Middle East and you are just someone who cares, but are not willing to go to extremes . . .' She drifted off. 'Then there is no future.'

She was thinking of moving to England with her husband, but, like Joyce, she felt a pull to remain in Palestine.

Dr Zakaria al-'Agha, who was one of the Palestinian delegates at the Madrid peace conference in 1991, saw a bigger problem with the next generation, the children who are still too young to comprehend the background of the intifada: 'The coming generation will have been born under occupation and will have seen violation of human rights and exploitation at every level,' he said. 'It is very deep in the hearts and the minds of these children. And this is why, when we meet foreign and Israeli politicians, we stress the importance of reaching a peaceful solution. Because if not now, it will become more and more difficult.'

There are the emotionally damaged, but there are also the physically damaged. In Beit Sahour the YMCA runs a rehabilitation centre for boys badly injured in the intifada; it is set in a stony shepherd's field near Bethlehem. The drive to Beit Sahour from Jerusalem, through twisting roads and the old hills, is so heart-breakingly beautiful that you could almost forget this is an occupied land in the middle of an uprising. But then reality returns when you pass the camps, or see the Israeli soldiers checking identity cards, or when your cab driver, who is Palestinian, has to leave his lights on so that you are not stoned by other Palestinians who might think you are Jews.

At the Beit Sahour centre I sat in a 'workshop' and watched teenage boys paint ceramic sculptures in garish colours – blue, red, violet, green. A plaster cast of Tom and Jerry. A cast of the Dome of the Rock Mosque. There was something too bizarre about the entire scene of boys with broken limbs and smashed-in faces painting useless objects.

'You like Tom and Jerry?' one of the boys, whose legs were twisted at a ninety-degree angle, asked as he limped over to me. His plaster cast was painted orange and black.

'It's very nice,' I said, and he limped off to show his friends.

'Very nice, she says,' he repeated in high-pitched English, 'very nice.'

Laila Atshan, the clinical social worker at Beit Sahour, was born blind. She was finishing her master's degree in America when she got a telephone call from the director of the YMCA asking if she could come to help set up a rehabilitation centre.

214

What disturbs her most is that this generation is completely unable to mourn. 'Like the mother who loses her child, but people in her camp are singing, "He's a martyr, he's a martyr." Well, that's bullshit,' Laila said fiercely, stamping out a cigarette. 'You have to be able to mourn, and the intifada does not allow these kids to do that.

'There is a sense of misdirection with these kids. There is something completely missing, and that is a sense of childhood. They don't live as children, they have to be little men from the time they're babies. When people have nothing to lose, life is meaningless. No role models, nothing to hope for. No teacher to teach them. There is no more challenge for them – the most exciting thing is to throw stones.'

As we walked up the stairs to the boys' rooms, Laila held on to my arm and ticked off the most common problems the boys have when they arrive at the centre. 'Fear of having relationships. Fear of rejection because they're disabled. Fear of the army. A lot of them have hysterical reactions. If they hear a sound like shooting or a tank, their immediate reaction is to run compulsively. In America, when you tell your children that they are safe, they are. Here, their fears are justified. Fear of being caught, beaten up, shot . . . what can I tell them?'

'Someone who has been incarcerated, tortured or badly injured goes through severe traumatic experiences,' said Dr Ahmed Baker. 'These children never regain the psychological balance that they once had. Their behaviour changes. Sometimes they become more submissive, sometimes more arrogant. But very often they are paranoid. They continue to behave as though they are in prison.'

The most common symptoms, Baker said, are nightmares, flashbacks and intense fear of Israeli soldiers. He said that part of the job of the Shin Bet once it has the activists in hand is to 'break them psychologically. The job is not complete until the person is completely submissive and dependent.' During interrogation this is accomplished in three ways: first, by making the prisoner dependent on the interrogator; secondly, by depriving them of sleep (according to Baker, the standard interrogation procedure is usually sleep deprivation of between thirty-six and forty-eight hours); and thirdly, by instilling in them a great dread.

'When they come to arrest a youth, they usually come at night, because it increases the sense of dread. They surround the door and bang on it, or break it open. Already you are destabilized. Next they disorientate them with hoods. Once the hoods are on the head and tied tightly, they drive around for about half an hour before taking them to prison.'

I have met several Palestinians who have been very badly tortured and who claim that they did not 'break'. Baker said that this is probably more damaging than when they do. 'It's almost like self-hypnosis, those that turn off the mind completely. I know of one man who was tortured severely, but refused to give in. He no longer speaks. The mind becomes an overloaded current. If you turn it off too much, there is a price to pay.'

Laila's therapy is to gather together a group of boys and try to get them to role-play, which, given the circumstances, has a slight air of absurdity. 'I tell them to be the soldier and to try to understand the soldier's mind, but sometimes all the psychology in the world can't help. I get so frustrated.'

Shadi, who was fourteen years old and wearing a *Friday the Thirteenth* T-shirt, entered the room and sat down awkwardly. He was tiny for his age, with long eyelashes – so long they almost looked false – but his face and demeanour were those of a sixty-year-old man. He told me, rather embarrassed, that he had been shot 'in the butt'. He stood up to demonstrate, lowering his trousers slightly over his hip, where the bullet went in, where it came out. The wound was the size of a small melon, angry, red and purple.

Shadi sat down and lit a cigarette. 'I was going upstairs in my house because I heard shooting outside the door, but the soldiers saw me and shot two dumdum bullets and two live bullets inside the house.'

He shrugged. 'No big deal,' he said. Everyone he knew had been shot or was dead.

I asked Shadi if he was sure they were dumdum bullets, which are designed to cause maximum damage. Whenever you ask Palestinian children what they were shot with, they will inevitably say 'dumdum' and go on to describe how the bullet pierces the skin and explodes inside the tissue or the organ. When you go to the Israeli Defence Force and ask them to explain why they were using dumdum bullets, they deny it. Doctors' reports vary constantly, but more times than not they will say that the injuries were inflicted by ammunition which is banned under the Geneva Convention. The matter was discussed in the *Daily Telegraph* on 26 January 1988:

'The x-rays taken of these injuries show clearly that the bullets have fragmented on impact,' said Mr Michael Lanigan, head of the delegation from the Parliamentary Association for European–Arab Cooperation and leader of the Irish Senate. 'Instead of causing a clean wound, the bullets are causing far more extensive damage. As a result, victims who in ordinary circumstances would make a full recovery will be maimed for life.'

And the London *Observer* reported on 10 January 1988:

Palestinian doctors in Gaza hospitals claim there is increasing evidence that the Army have been using exploding dum-dum bullets to fire on rioters from these camps. The senior registrar of the Shifa Hospital in Gaza city said: 'On many of our x-rays we find shrapnel inside the patient. Sometimes we find one bullet with 10 pieces of shrapnel and I can assure you these are not rubber bullets.'

Shadi insisted he was shot by a dumdum. He described in detail the sensation when the bullet went in and when the doctors cut into him. There was no emotion as he talked; he simply smoked and gave a clinical report. 'It felt like fire going through my skin, and then I looked down and saw the blood and then I put my hand over the wound.' Laila blanched and distracted him by asking, 'What do you want to do when you get out of here, when you grow up?' He blushed, reached over and whispered something in her ear. 'He says he wants to get married.'

'And do you want to work? What kind of work do you want to do?'

He laughed and said nothing, but Laila pressed him. 'All right,' Shadi said. 'A hobo. A street person. Then I won't have to think about the intifada.'

Taher came in, smiling, a pair of phoney Ray-Bans propped up on his nose. He was eighteen years old and had been shot near his optic nerve on his way to the mosque. He had lost sight in both eyes.

'Were you throwing stones? The soldiers said that you were throwing stones.'

He shook his head. He was still smiling, and I asked him if he felt bitter about the shooting. 'Bitter? Not bitter.' He was religious and believed it was God's fate. When I asked what he would do to support himself – he was a barber before the incident – he answered slowly, 'Only God knows.' There was a sense of calmness about him, odd for one who lost his sight at the age of eighteen. He said he was not political, but then, all the boys said they were not political. The word simply does not mean the same to them as it does to us. 'His first priority,' Leila added, 'is to learn Braille to read. Then to find something suitable for his situation. To become independent.'

The newest extension at Beit Sahour is the wheelchair section. She called it the 'quadriplegic' area and said she did not like to go there as it depressed her and she didn't like the smell; but she took my arm and we walked to the squat building which was set slightly apart from the others. 'It makes me too sad. Last week one of the counsellors had to go and take one of the boys into the shower, he was completely covered in shit.' She tripped slightly on a stone and steadied herself. 'I can't stand it when I think that these kids were completely healthy one year, two years ago. Now they can't walk, they can't see, they will have pain for the rest of their lives. And for what?' Her mouth set in a rigid line. 'I get so angry.'

Inside the whitewashed room there were three boys, two in beds and one in a wheelchair, slapping flies off of his legs. All of them had been shot in or near the spinal cord. One, about seventeen, was naked from the waist up. He reached for the sheet to cover himself, and said that he had just arrived and did not feel like talking. He moved his legs into the centre of the bed with his hands, grimacing as he did so. The boy in the wheelchair came over and adjusted the blanket over his legs. He lit a cigarette and placed it in his friend's mouth. Then he wheeled his chair closer to me and addressed me in English. 'Hello, how are you?' But he was scowling.

The smallest one, Waleed, was twenty-one, and married with two children. For someone lying in bed unable to move his legs, he had a remarkably good sense of humour. 'I'm a Communist Muslim!' he said, laughing. Unlike the others, he admitted to being political and told me about the shooting in graphic detail.

'And then the bullet went into my back, and I felt it come out and then I felt . . .' He said he was walking to a demonstration and yes, he threw a stone at a soldier. 'I did it for the intifada. Now, of course, I am paying a very big price for it.' He pointed at his useless legs under the mound of sheets.

'What are you going to do when you get out of here?'

Blank stare. A look of confusion. He dragged on his cigarette. Then a thought occurred to him and his eyes lit up. 'Maybe I'll run a video shop.'

I am ending with the stories of the next generation because I began with the next generation, the old Arab who told David Grossman about the fate of his grandchildren's grandchildren. Eventually, though no one is quite sure when, the intifada will end with or without a political solution. At the moment, in the wake of the new government, there seems to be hope that something can be resolved. Even then, there will be a whole generation of Israelis and Palestinians left to deal with its shattering impact. Mary Khass believes that the most important thing is to show the children beauty and security now, especially the small ones who see only injury and destruction, and to try to teach them to use their imaginations to see a better life, in time.

Children need privacy, but in the camps there are, on average, seven people to a room. Khass told me this in a quiet voice as we sat on the veranda of Marna House, the only real hotel in the Gaza Strip. She was thoughtful and resigned, and then she thought of something and burst out laughing. 'One time I was leading a story group with little children, three- to five-year-olds. I started a story and I wanted them to finish it. "This summer," I said in an enthusiastic voice, "this summer we're all going to go to Egypt. And when we go to Egypt, we are going to go to the zoo. And what do we see in the zoo?"'

Mary called on Ahmed, one of her favourite children, to answer. He refused. When she pushed him, he looked up and said slowly, 'We can't go to Egypt because we haven't got the exit permits.' Mary Khass's face dropped. 'And that to me is the most tragic thing. That these children have lost the ability to imagine.'

There is an image that always enters my head when I think of children and the intifada. It comes from one of my earliest trips to the West Bank, at the beginning of the intifada, to the first refugee camp that I visited – Jalazon, near Jerusalem. I remember meeting four small boys, maybe ten years old, who came out to say goodbye to me as I backed my car out of the camp. They stood in front of a home demolished by the army and covered in angry black graffiti, waving and flashing me the V-for-victory sign. One of them had found a frog and he held it up and waved it at me, like a farewell sign.

As I was driving back through the Jewish settlements, I thought how strange, how out of place that frog looked because it was something a normal group of ten-year-olds would play with. But this was not a normal group of ten-year-olds. This was the West Bank, this was the intifada, and statistics suggest that one of the four would not live to be eighteen.

Appendix: Key Dates
in the History of Palestine and Israel

By 8000 BC	Small groups of hunter gatherers have settled in permanent communities in Palestine. Jericho is one such early settlement.
By 3000	The land is called Canaan and the people Canaanites.
c. 1700	The Hyksos people invade from the east and conquer Canaan and Egypt. Many Hyksos, including the ancestors of the Hebrews, settle in Canaan.
c. 1600	Egypt drives out the Hyksos and controls Canaan.
c. 1300	The Canaanites regain their independence.
1100s	The Philistines invade from the west and three groups of Hebrews invade from the east. Simultaneously a Hebrew tribe, the Israelites, returns to Canaan from Egypt. Together the Hebrews defeat the Canaanites. The Philistines establish many coastal settlements. Gaza is one of their greatest cities.
1020	King Saul unites the Israeli tribes into one kingdom.
900s	Kings David and Solomon bring Israel to the peak of its power and wealth.
700s–300s	The Babylonian, Persian and Syrian empires control the region.
586	The Babylonians destroy Jerusalem and scatter most of the Hebrews through Babylonia and Egypt. Those remaining are known as Jews from this point.
300s–c. 1	The region is ruled by Alexander the Great, then by Egyptian and Turkish–Syrian empires. Jewish leaders

	resist other invaders and re-establish an independent Hebrew kingdom.
63	Rome captures Palestine. The Jews revolt unsuccessfully.
AD 70	Jerusalem is destroyed, forcing a national migration out of Palestine.
132	The Romans crush the Jewish revolt. Most surviving Jews flee to neighbouring countries, ending Jewish power in Palestine.
300s–600s	Palestine belongs to the Western Roman Empire and later to the Byzantine Empire. The population grows and Christianity becomes the main religion of the region.
571	Muhammed is thought to have been born.
638–40	Palestine is conquered by Muslim warriors from Arabia and becomes a centre of Arab culture and commerce. Arab Muslims gradually dominate the population.
1095	The First Crusade recaptures Palestine from the Arabs.
1099	The crusaders capture Jerusalem and set up a Christian state called the Kingdom of Jerusalem, which includes the West Bank and the Gaza Strip.
By 1291	Muslim Arabs have driven out the last crusaders.
1300s–1400s	Palestine declines through a century of drought, plague and economic stagnation.
1516	The Ottoman Empire conquers Palestine and begins its 400-year rule.
1801	Napoleon Bonaparte captures Gaza, but is repulsed by British and Ottoman forces.
1831–40	Muhammed Ali, the Ottoman governor of Egypt, rules Palestine.
Late 1800s	Jewish settlers from Germany, France and Russia set up colonies in thinly populated areas of Palestine.
1897	The First Zionist Congress is organized in Basle by

	Theodor Herzl, founder of political Zionism. It calls for the colonization of Palestine by Jews.
1917	The Balfour Declaration states that the British government favours 'the establishment in Palestine of a National Home for the Jewish people' and will work for its achievement on the grounds that 'nothing shall be done which may prejudice the civil and religious rights of existing non-Jewish communities in Palestine'.
1917–18	Britain defeats Ottoman forces in the First World War and captures Palestine.
1920	Britain receives the Palestinian mandate, with the obligation to carry out the terms of the Balfour Declaration. Thousands of Jewish immigrants arrive. Resentment and violence simmer between Jews and Arabs.
1923–9	Jewish immigration comes to a virtual standstill.
1929	Britain agrees to enlarge the Jewish Agency, a kind of autonomous Jewish government within Palestine. There are severe clashes between Jews and Arabs in Jerusalem.
1930–35	There is a sharp rise in immigration as Hitler comes to power.
1936–8	The Arabs organize a rebellion against the British mandate.
1939	The British government's white paper limits Jewish immigration and sets out the establishment of an independent state of Palestine within ten years. The Zionists see it as a betrayal of the Balfour Declaration.
1939–45	Haganah is formed as an underground Zionist army, with Irgun and the Stern Gang breaking away as extreme factions. There are widespread attacks on British targets.
1948	Britain's formal withdrawal from Palestine results in civil war. Zionist resistance groups unite to capture

Palestine. Arab morale is crushed by their superior force and by the massacre of 250 villagers in Deir Yassin. Major towns and Arab-controlled Jerusalem fall. Thousands of Arab refugees pour into neighbouring regions.

The mandate formally ends on 14 May and the Zionists, led by Chaim Weizmann, proclaim the foundation of the state of Israel. The next day pan-Arab forces cross the borders to reclaim Palestine.

1949   The War of Independence ends with seventy-nine per cent of Palestine in Jewish control. Egypt keeps the Gaza Strip, but Jerusalem is split into Arab East and Jewish West.

1950s   The Law of Return brings in hundreds of thousands of Jews from Eastern Europe and Arab states.

1956   Israel invades Sinai and captures the Gaza Strip, but returns it to Egyptian control in 1957.

1963   Arab heads of state agree to set up the Palestine Liberation Organization, with its own army, to represent the Palestinian people. Al-Fatah, the Palestinian military resistance movement, is founded and begins to carry out operations against Israel from Jordan and Syria.

1967   The Six Day War. Egypt enters Sinai and closes the Straits of Tiran to Israeli shipping. Israel destroys most of Egypt's air force and defeats the army in Sinai. Israel controls all of Jerusalem and the remaining twenty-one per cent of Palestine. Yasser Arafat becomes spokesman for Al-Fatah.

1969   Arafat becomes chairman of the PLO.

1973   The Yom Kippur War. Egypt and Syria attack Israel with much initial success. With emergency arms aid from America, Israel pushes Syria back and advances to within eighty kilometres of Cairo. A peace settlement is negotiated and the Gaza Strip and the West Bank remain in Israeli control. Victory won at such a high cost to life causes domestic anger, and there is a ground swell of support for the opposition right-wing Likud Party.

1974   Arafat is accorded the honours of a head of state when he speaks to the United Nations to urge the world to recognize the rights of the homeless Palestinians.

1977–8   President Sadat of Egypt makes an unprecedented speech to the Knesset and calls for tolerance and equality between Jews and Arabs. Peace negotiations begin at Camp David in America.

1979   A two-part peace treaty is agreed: the restoration of Egyptian rule over its territory and the normalization of relations with Israel; the provision of ultimate self-government for the occupied territories over five years.

1982   Israel evacuates Sinai and the Israeli–Egyptian border is opened. Israel invades Lebanon to try to destroy the PLO base there. Beirut is besieged for two months; thousands are killed and made homeless. America intervenes to allow the PLO to flee to other Arab countries. Massacres of Palestinian civilians in Sabra and Shatila refugee camps by Lebanese Phalangist militiamen are not prevented by the controlling Israeli forces. The biggest ever political rally in Israel is held in protest over the killings.

1983   Syrian-backed rebels within the PLO denounce Arafat for appearing willing to negotiate with Israel. The PLO decamps to Tunis.

1985   Israeli forces are withdrawn from Lebanon. An Israeli air raid on its headquarters in Tunis fails to destroy the PLO.

Appendix

1987   The intifada begins.

1988   The Palestine National Council (the quasi-parliament in exile) officially recognizes Israel. The PLO renounces terrorism.

1991   Peace talks are opened between Israeli and Palestinian representatives in the aftermath of the Gulf War.

1992   Yitzak Rabin's Labour Party ends fifteen years of right-wing Likud Party rule in the general election, promising to put a freeze on new settlements and to allow Palestinian autonomy in the occupied territories.